'The old world is dying,
and the new world struggles
to be born: now is the
time of monsters'.

- Antonio Gramsci -

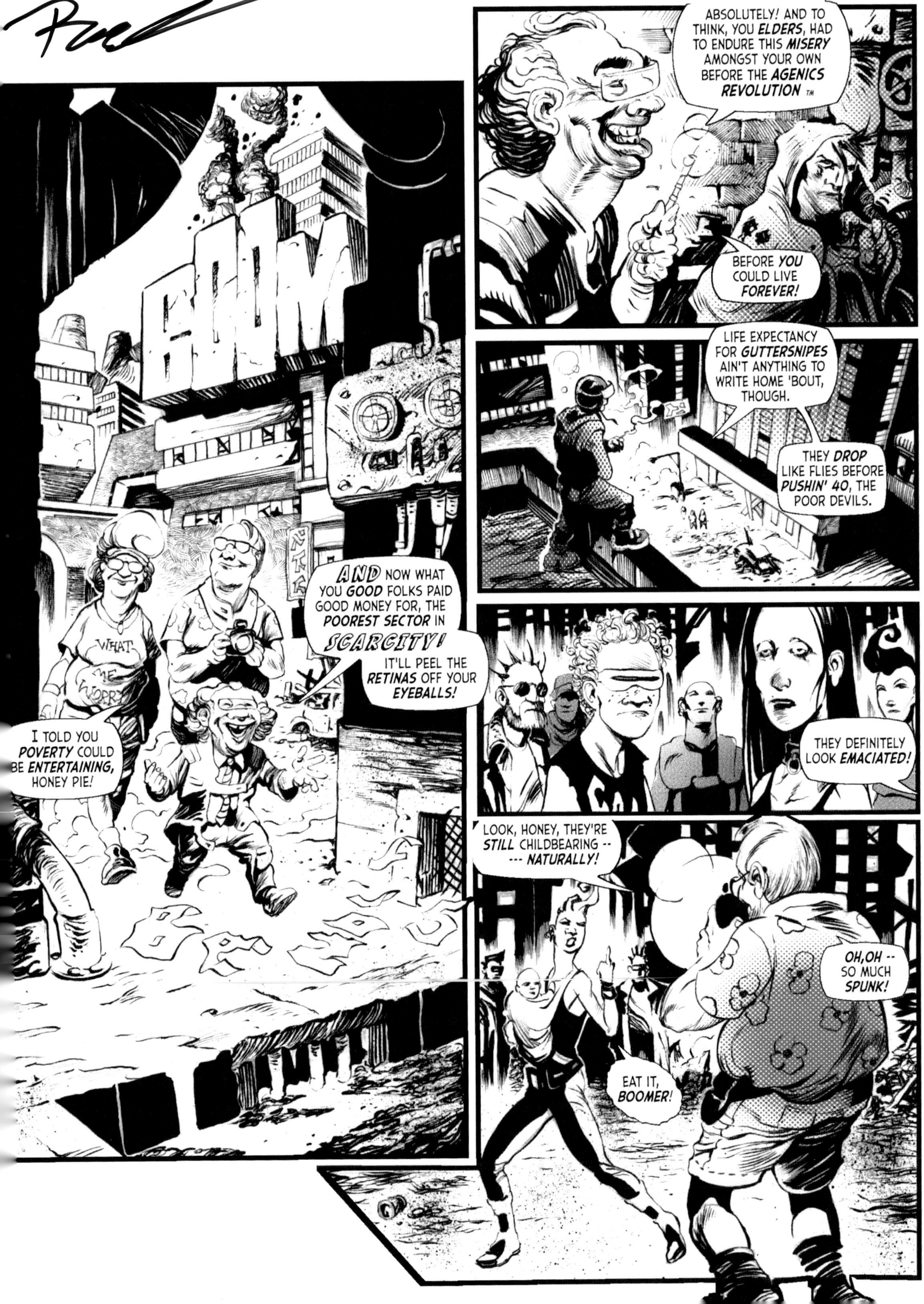
BOOM
AND NOW WHAT YOU GOOD FOLKS PAID GOOD MONEY FOR, THE POOREST SECTOR IN SCARCITY!
IT'LL PEEL THE RETINAS OFF YOUR EYEBALLS!
I TOLD YOU POVERTY COULD BE ENTERTAINING, HONEY PIE!
ABSOLUTELY! AND TO THINK, YOU ELDERS, HAD TO ENDURE THIS MISERY AMONGST YOUR OWN BEFORE THE AGENICS REVOLUTION TM
BEFORE YOU COULD LIVE FOREVER!
LIFE EXPECTANCY FOR GUTTERSNIPES AIN'T ANYTHING TO WRITE HOME 'BOUT, THOUGH.
THEY DROP LIKE FLIES BEFORE PUSHIN' 40, THE POOR DEVILS.
THEY DEFINITELY LOOK EMACIATED!
LOOK, HONEY, THEY'RE STILL CHILDBEARING -- --- NATURALLY!
OH,OH -- SO MUCH SPUNK!
EAT IT, BOOMER!

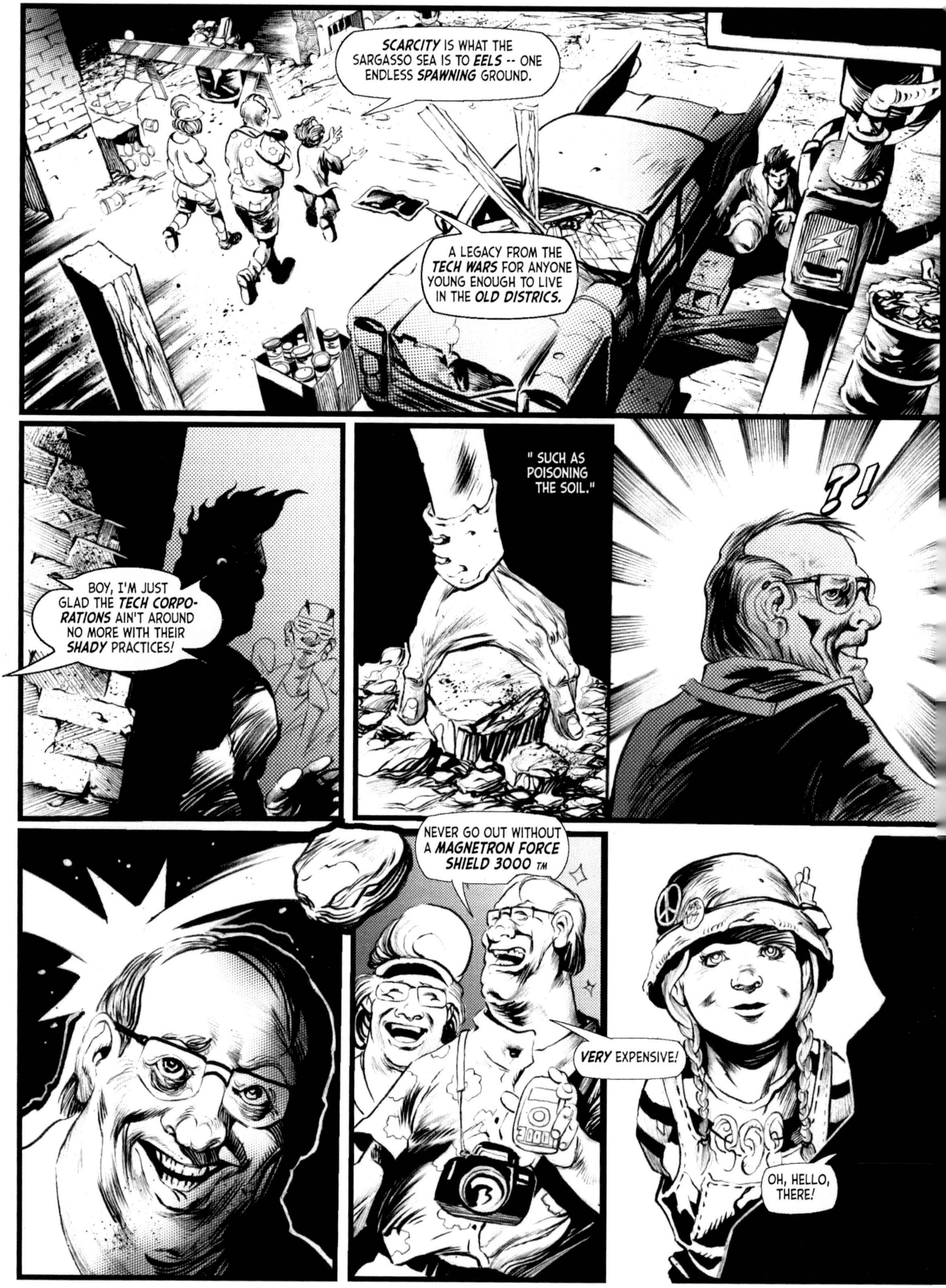
SCARCITY IS WHAT THE SARGASSO SEA IS TO EELS -- ONE ENDLESS SPAWNING GROUND.
A LEGACY FROM THE TECH WARS FOR ANYONE YOUNG ENOUGH TO LIVE IN THE OLD DISTRICS.
BOY, I'M JUST GLAD THE TECH CORPO-RATIONS AIN'T AROUND NO MORE WITH THEIR SHADY PRACTICES!
" SUCH AS POISONING THE SOIL."
?!
NEVER GO OUT WITHOUT A MAGNETRON FORCE SHIELD 3000 TM
VERY EXPENSIVE!
OH, HELLO, THERE!

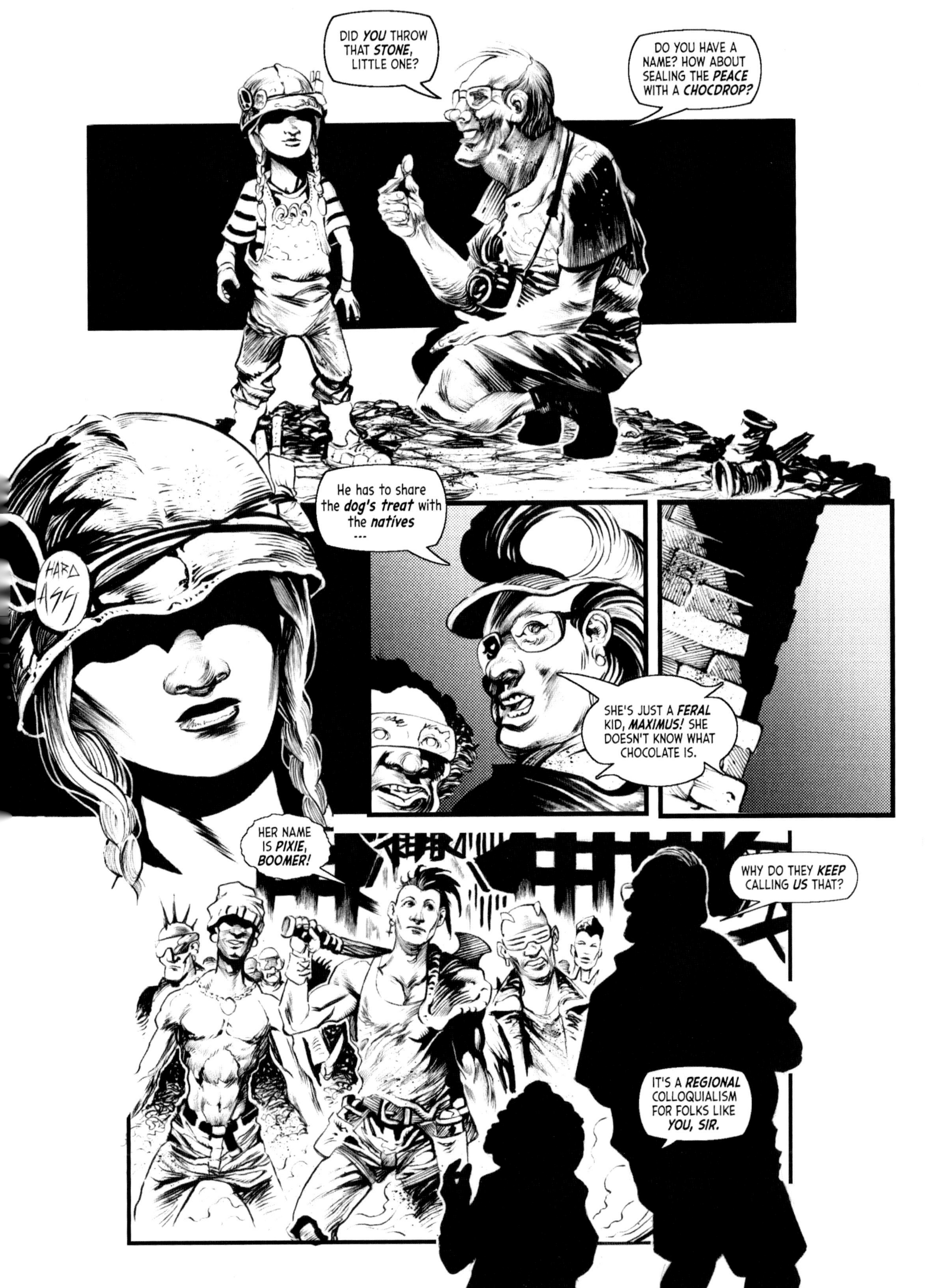
DID YOU THROW THAT STONE, LITTLE ONE?
DO YOU HAVE A NAME? HOW ABOUT SEALING THE PEACE WITH A CHOCDROP?
He has to share the dog's treat with the natives ---
HARD ASS
SHE'S JUST A FERAL KID, MAXIMUS! SHE DOESN'T KNOW WHAT CHOCOLATE IS.
HER NAME IS PIXIE, BOOMER!
WHY DO THEY KEEP CALLING US THAT?
IT'S A REGIONAL COLLOQUIALISM FOR FOLKS LIKE YOU, SIR.

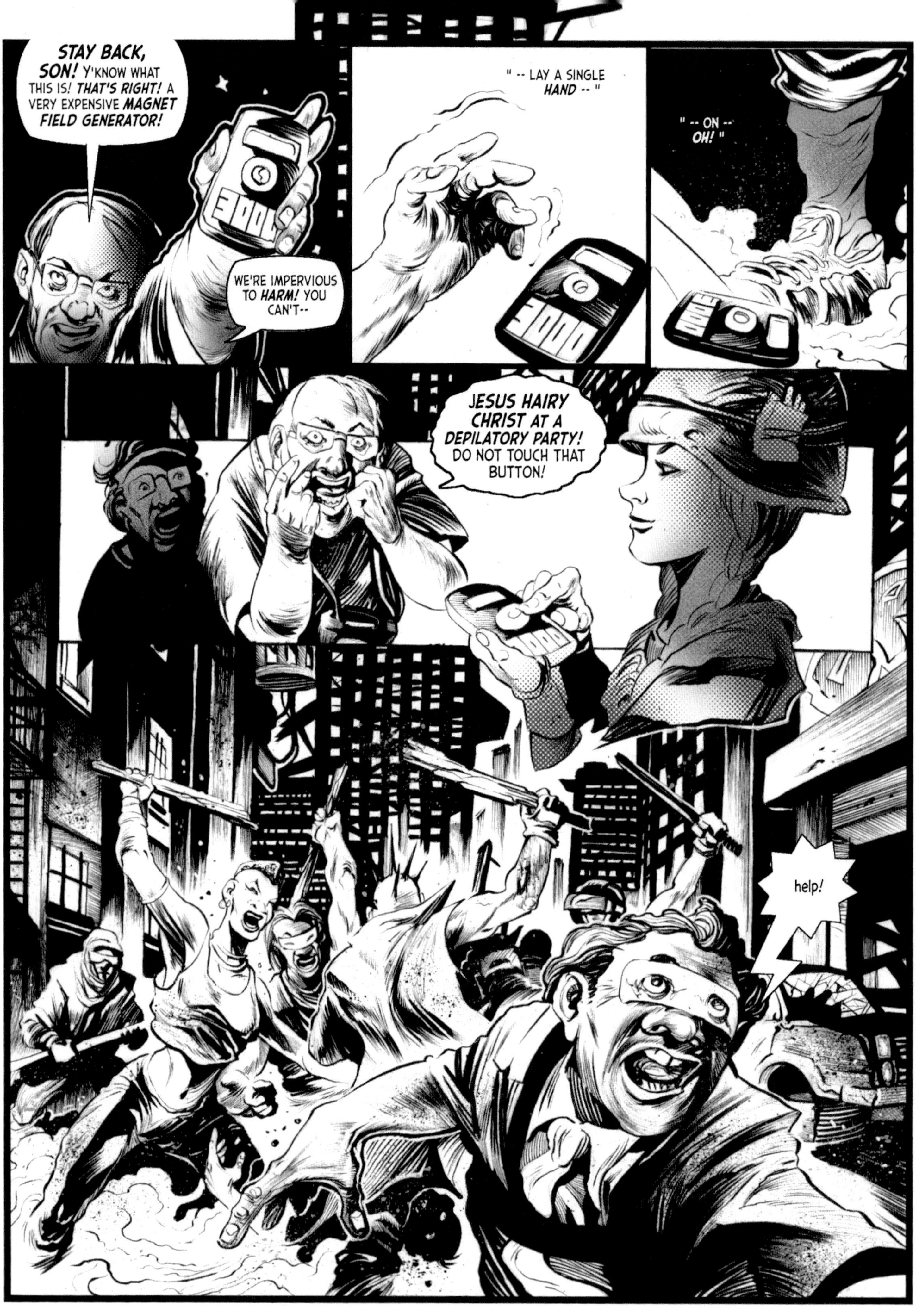
STAY BACK, SON! Y'KNOW WHAT THIS IS! THAT'S RIGHT! A VERY EXPENSIVE MAGNET FIELD GENERATOR!
WE'RE IMPERVIOUS TO HARM! YOU CAN'T--
" -- LAY A SINGLE HAND -- "
" -- ON -- OH! "
JESUS HAIRY CHRIST AT A DEPILATORY PARTY! DO NOT TOUCH THAT BUTTON!
help!

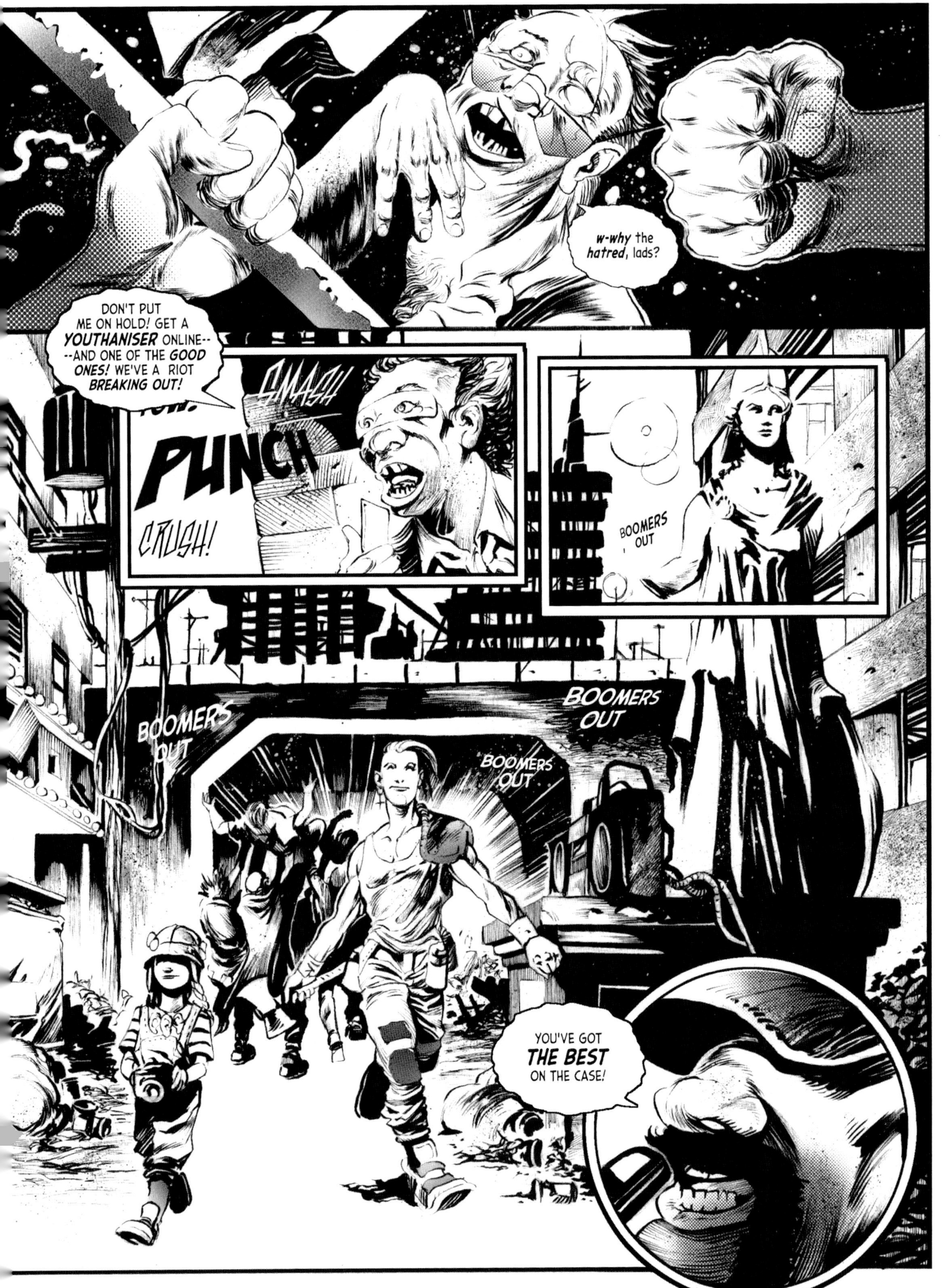

w-why the hatred, lads?
DON'T PUT ME ON HOLD! GET A YOUTHANISER ONLINE-- --AND ONE OF THE GOOD ONES! WE'VE A RIOT BREAKING OUT!
SMASH
PUNCH
CRUSH!
BOOMERS OUT
BOOMERS OUT
BOOMERS OUT
BOOMERS OUT
YOU'VE GOT THE BEST ON THE CASE!

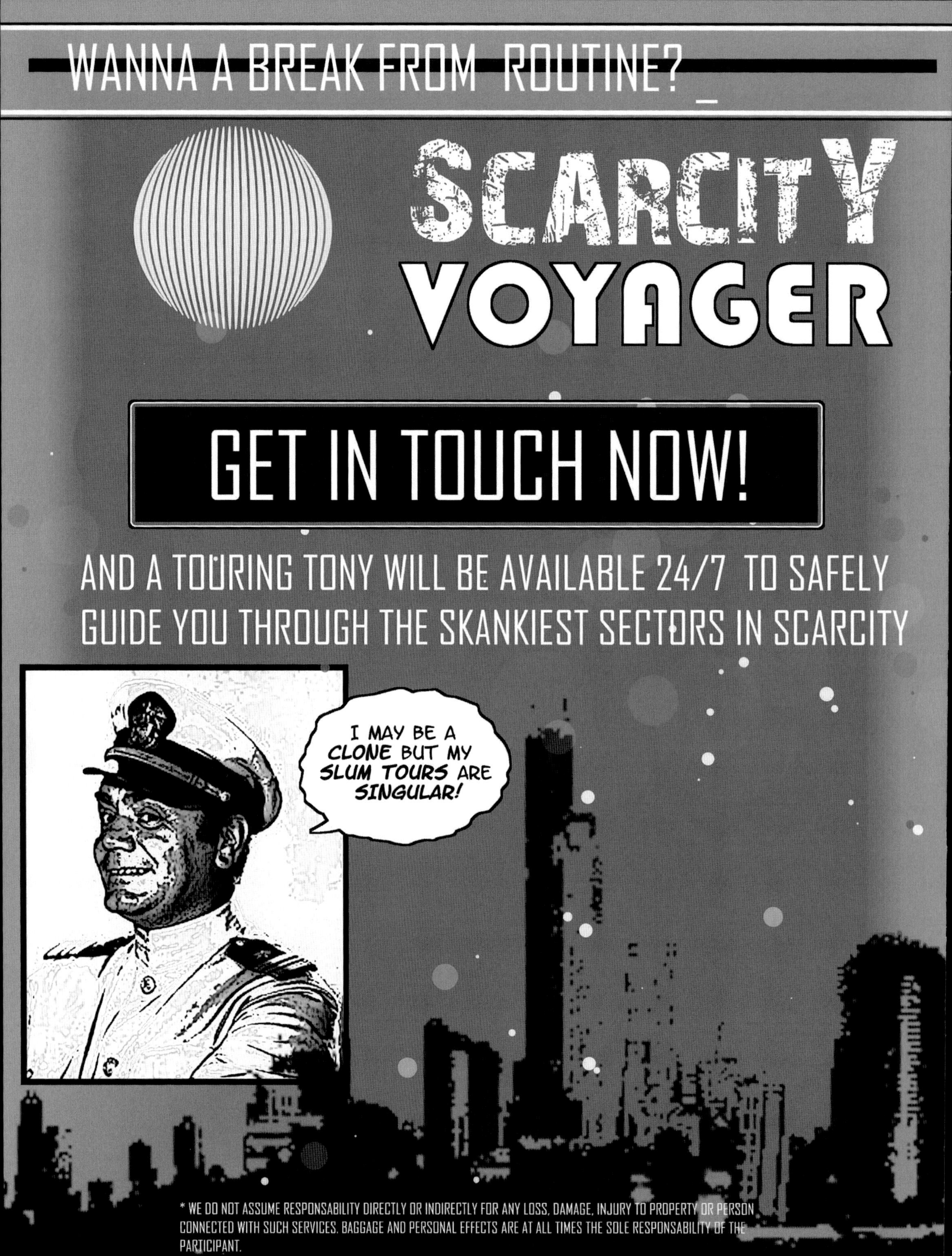

WANNA A BREAK FROM ROUTINE? _
SCARCITY VOYAGER
GET IN TOUCH NOW!
AND A TOURING TONY WILL BE AVAILABLE 24/7 TO SAFELY GUIDE YOU THROUGH THE SKANKIEST SECTORS IN SCARCITY
I MAY BE A CLONE BUT MY SLUM TOURS ARE SINGULAR!
* WE DO NOT ASSUME RESPONSABILITY DIRECTLY OR INDIRECTLY FOR ANY LOSS, DAMAGE, INJURY TO PROPERTY OR PERSON CONNECTED WITH SUCH SERVICES. BAGGAGE AND PERSONAL EFFECTS ARE AT ALL TIMES THE SOLE RESPONSABILITY OF THE PARTICIPANT.

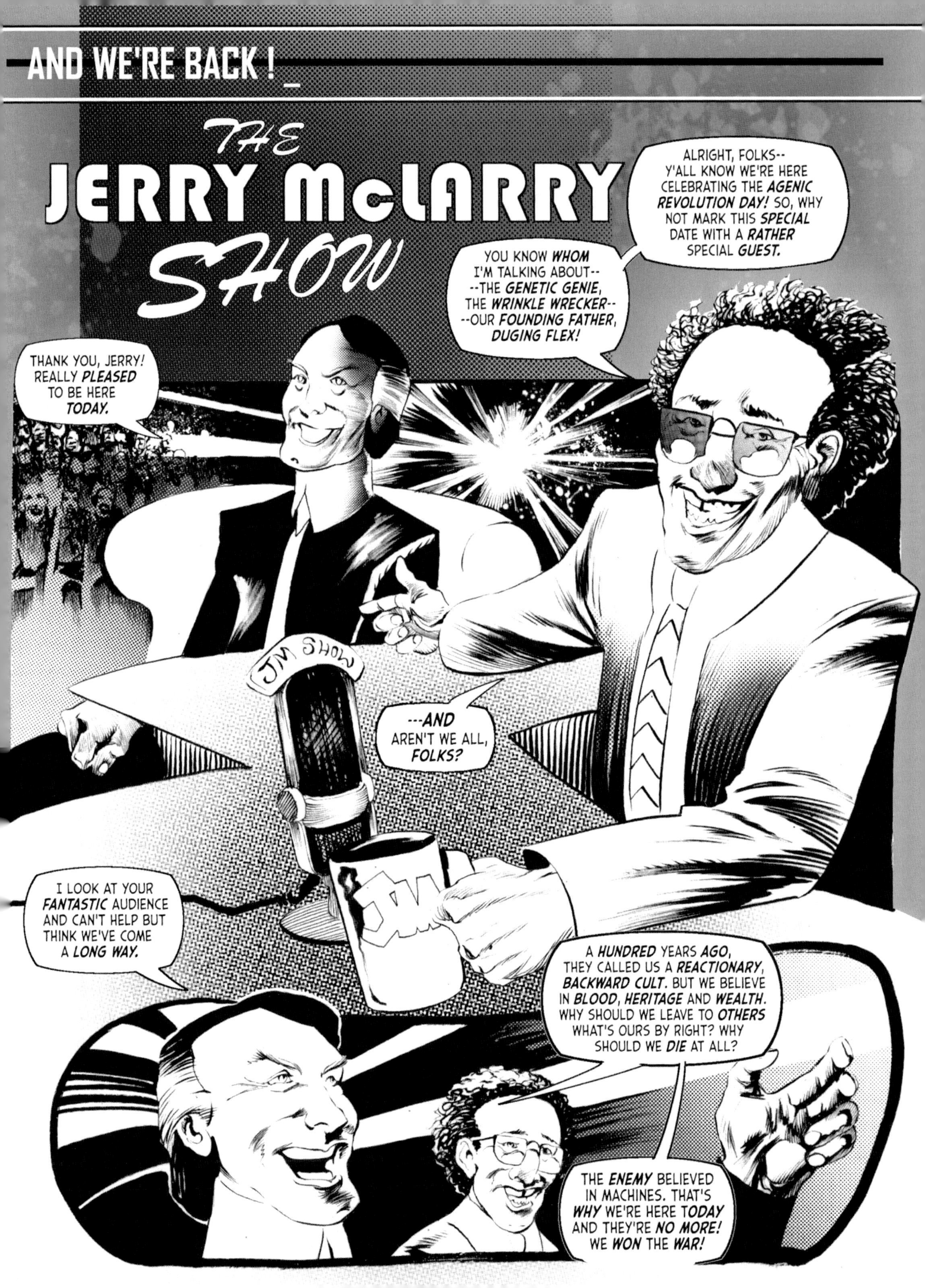
AND WE'RE BACK !
THE JERRY McLARRY SHOW
ALRIGHT, FOLKS-- Y'ALL KNOW WE'RE HERE CELEBRATING THE AGENIC REVOLUTION DAY! SO, WHY NOT MARK THIS SPECIAL DATE WITH A RATHER SPECIAL GUEST.
YOU KNOW WHOM I'M TALKING ABOUT-- --THE GENETIC GENIE, THE WRINKLE WRECKER-- --OUR FOUNDING FATHER, DUGING FLEX!
THANK YOU, JERRY! REALLY PLEASED TO BE HERE TODAY.
JM SHOW
---AND AREN'T WE ALL, FOLKS?
I LOOK AT YOUR FANTASTIC AUDIENCE AND CAN'T HELP BUT THINK WE'VE COME A LONG WAY.
A HUNDRED YEARS AGO, THEY CALLED US A REACTIONARY, BACKWARD CULT. BUT WE BELIEVE IN BLOOD, HERITAGE AND WEALTH. WHY SHOULD WE LEAVE TO OTHERS WHAT'S OURS BY RIGHT? WHY SHOULD WE DIE AT ALL?
THE ENEMY BELIEVED IN MACHINES. THAT'S WHY WE'RE HERE TODAY AND THEY'RE NO MORE! WE WON THE WAR!

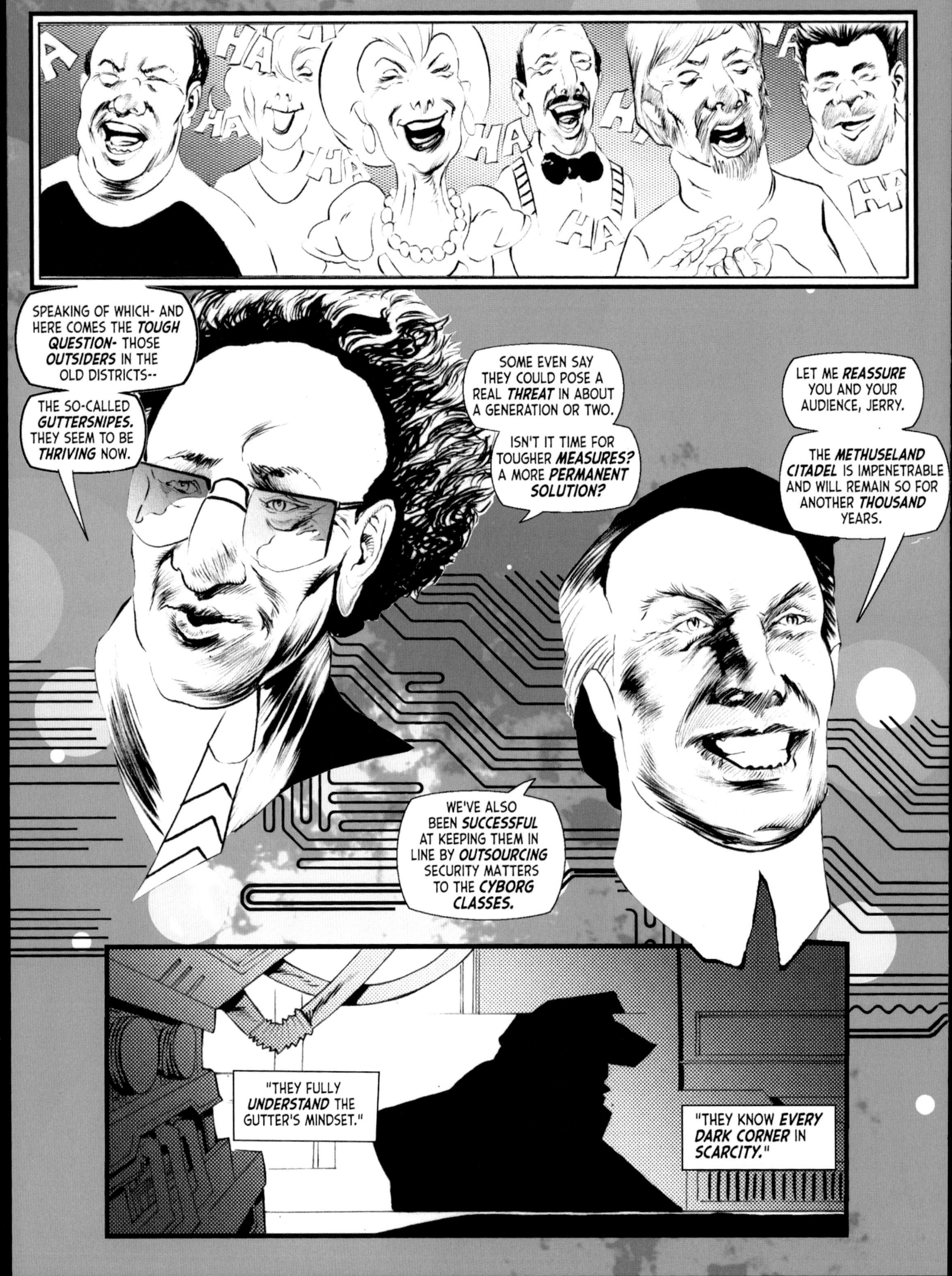
HA HA HA HA HA HA HA HA HA HA
SPEAKING OF WHICH- AND HERE COMES THE TOUGH QUESTION- THOSE OUTSIDERS IN THE OLD DISTRICTS--
THE SO-CALLED GUTTERSNIPES. THEY SEEM TO BE THRIVING NOW.
SOME EVEN SAY THEY COULD POSE A REAL THREAT IN ABOUT A GENERATION OR TWO.
ISN'T IT TIME FOR TOUGHER MEASURES? A MORE PERMANENT SOLUTION?
LET ME REASSURE YOU AND YOUR AUDIENCE, JERRY.
THE METHUSELAND CITADEL IS IMPENETRABLE AND WILL REMAIN SO FOR ANOTHER THOUSAND YEARS.
WE'VE ALSO BEEN SUCCESSFUL AT KEEPING THEM IN LINE BY OUTSOURCING SECURITY MATTERS TO THE CYBORG CLASSES.
"THEY FULLY UNDERSTAND THE GUTTER'S MINDSET."
"THEY KNOW EVERY DARK CORNER IN SCARCITY."

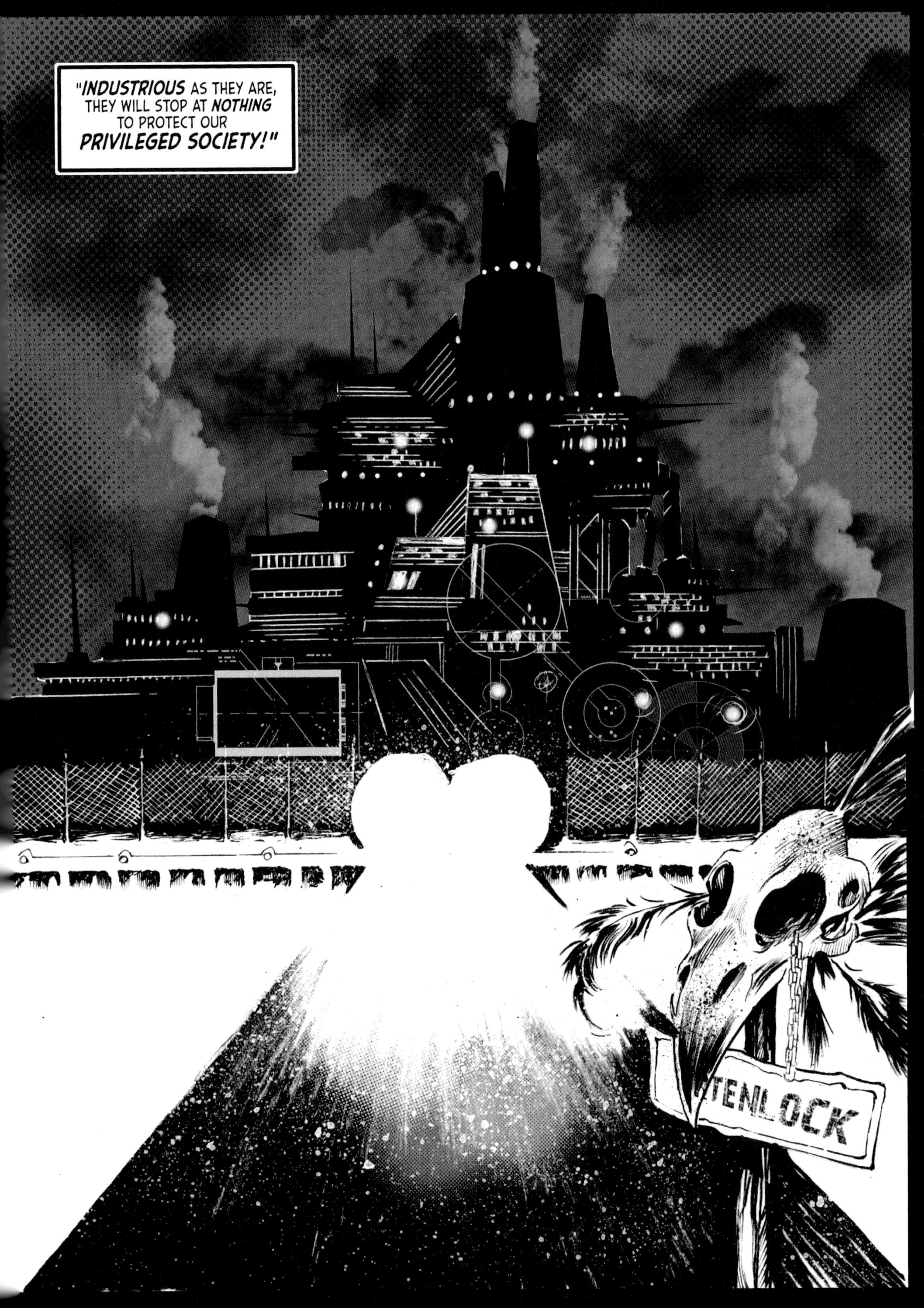
"INDUSTRIOUS AS THEY ARE, THEY WILL STOP AT NOTHING TO PROTECT OUR PRIVILEGED SOCIETY!"
TENLOCK

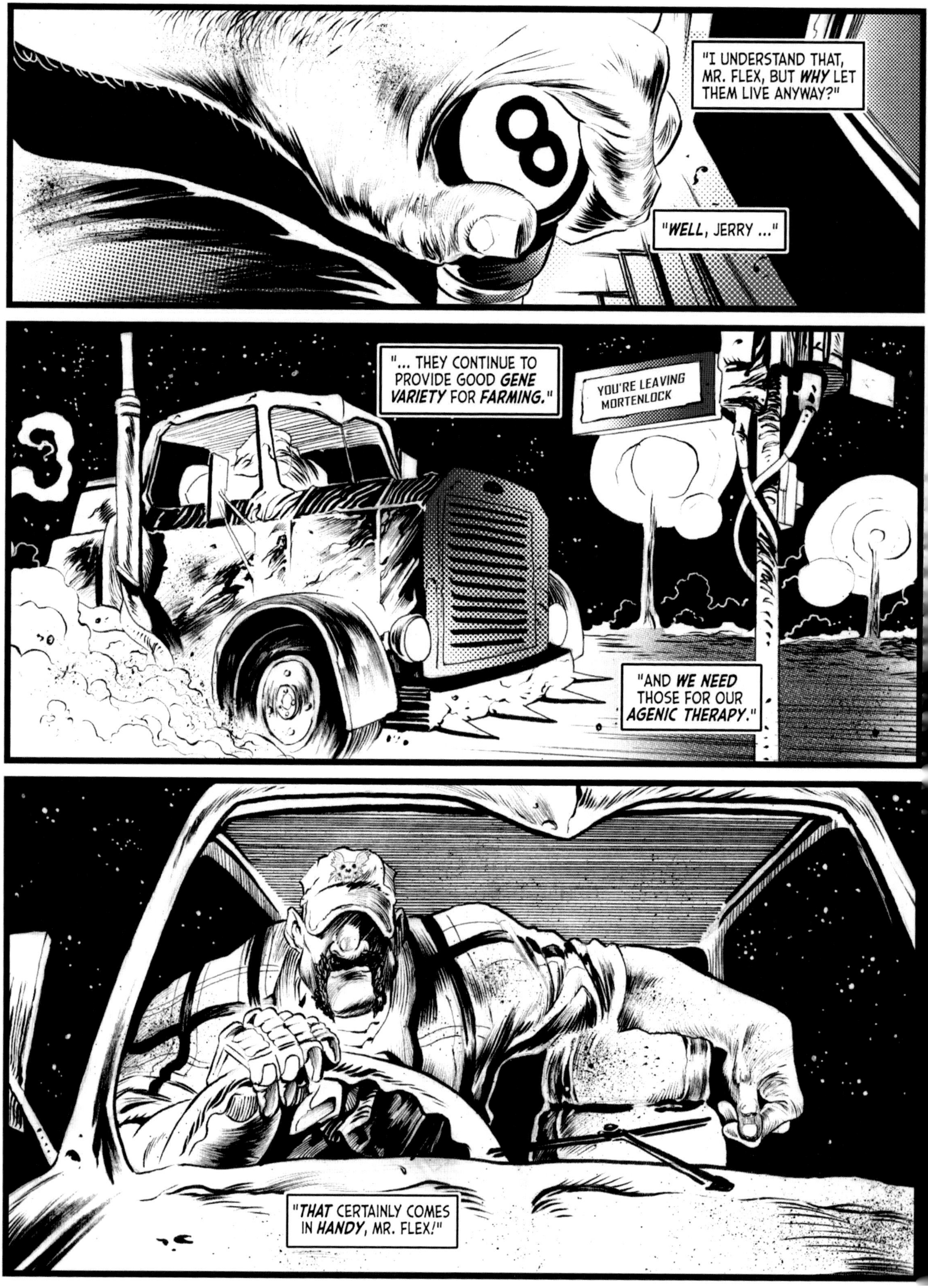
"I UNDERSTAND THAT, MR. FLEX, BUT WHY LET THEM LIVE ANYWAY?"
"WELL, JERRY ..."
"... THEY CONTINUE TO PROVIDE GOOD GENE VARIETY FOR FARMING."
YOU'RE LEAVING MORTENLOCK
"AND WE NEED THOSE FOR OUR AGENIC THERAPY."
"THAT CERTAINLY COMES IN HANDY, MR. FLEX!"

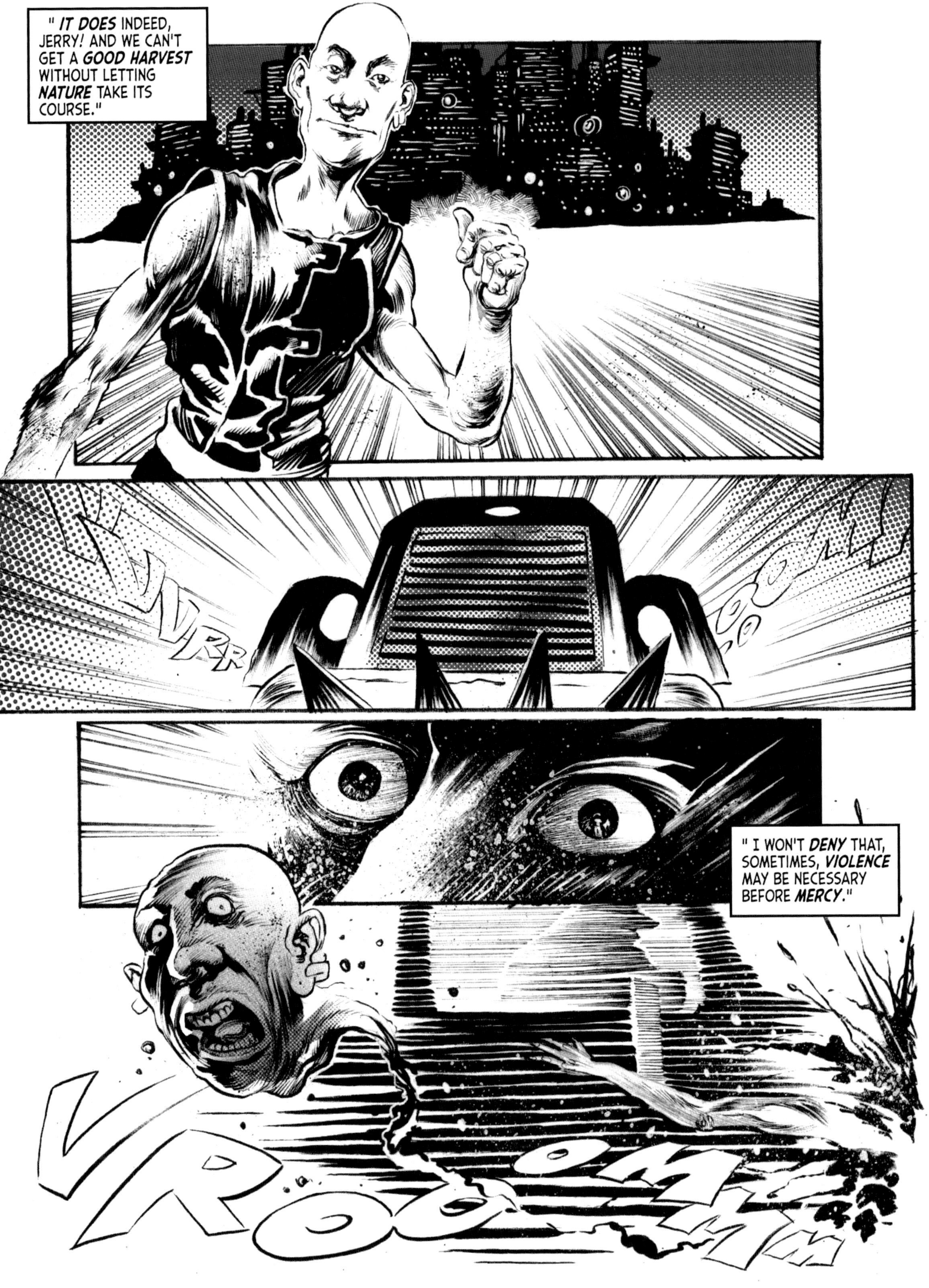
" IT DOES INDEED, JERRY! AND WE CAN'T GET A GOOD HARVEST WITHOUT LETTING NATURE TAKE ITS COURSE."
" I WON'T DENY THAT, SOMETIMES, VIOLENCE MAY BE NECESSARY BEFORE MERCY."

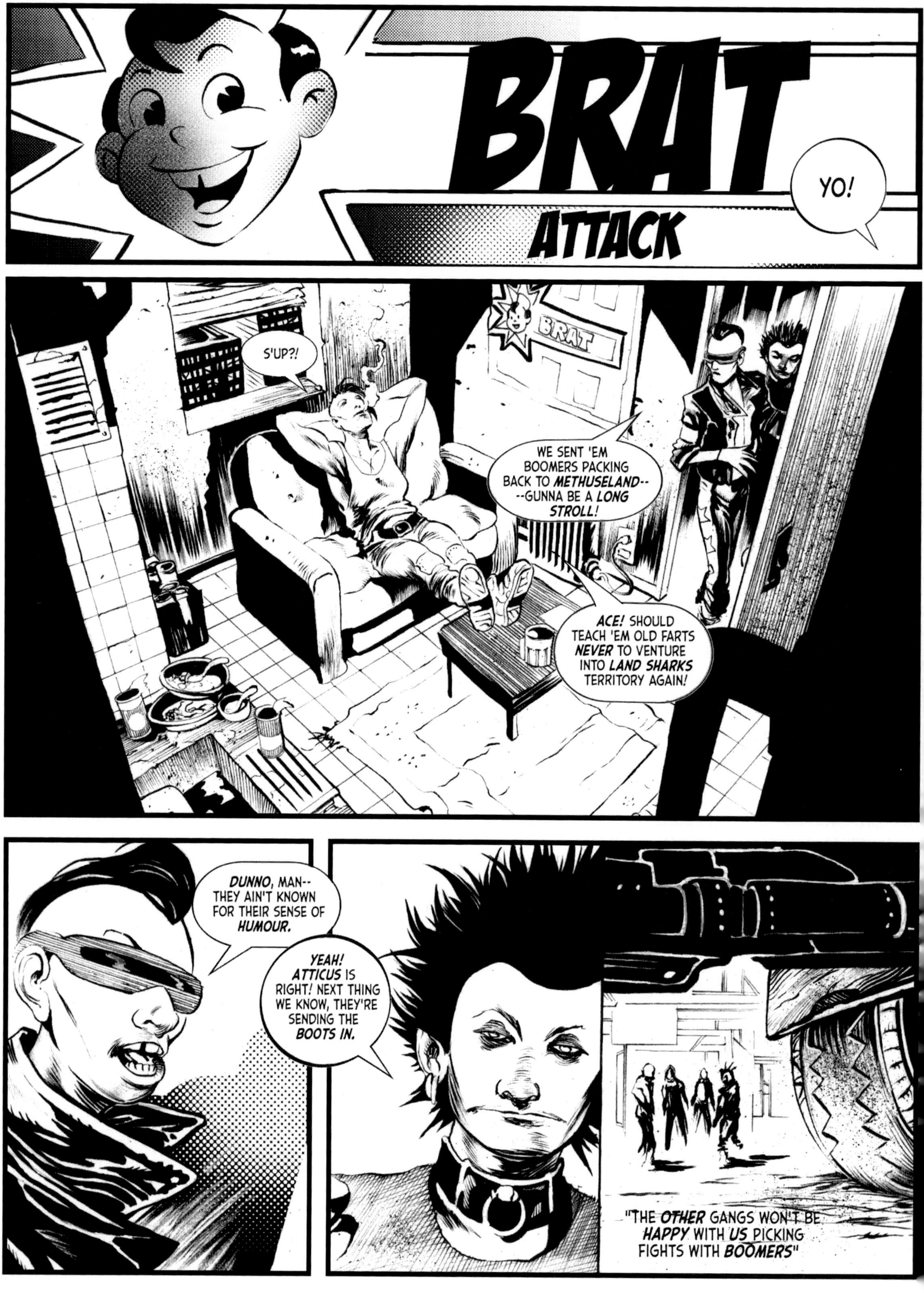
BRAT ATTACK
YO!
S'UP?!
WE SENT 'EM BOOMERS PACKING BACK TO METHUSELAND--
--GUNNA BE A LONG STROLL!
ACE! SHOULD TEACH 'EM OLD FARTS NEVER TO VENTURE INTO LAND SHARKS TERRITORY AGAIN!
DUNNO, MAN-- THEY AIN'T KNOWN FOR THEIR SENSE OF HUMOUR.
YEAH! ATTICUS IS RIGHT! NEXT THING WE KNOW, THEY'RE SENDING THE BOOTS IN.
"THE OTHER GANGS WON'T BE HAPPY WITH US PICKING FIGHTS WITH BOOMERS"

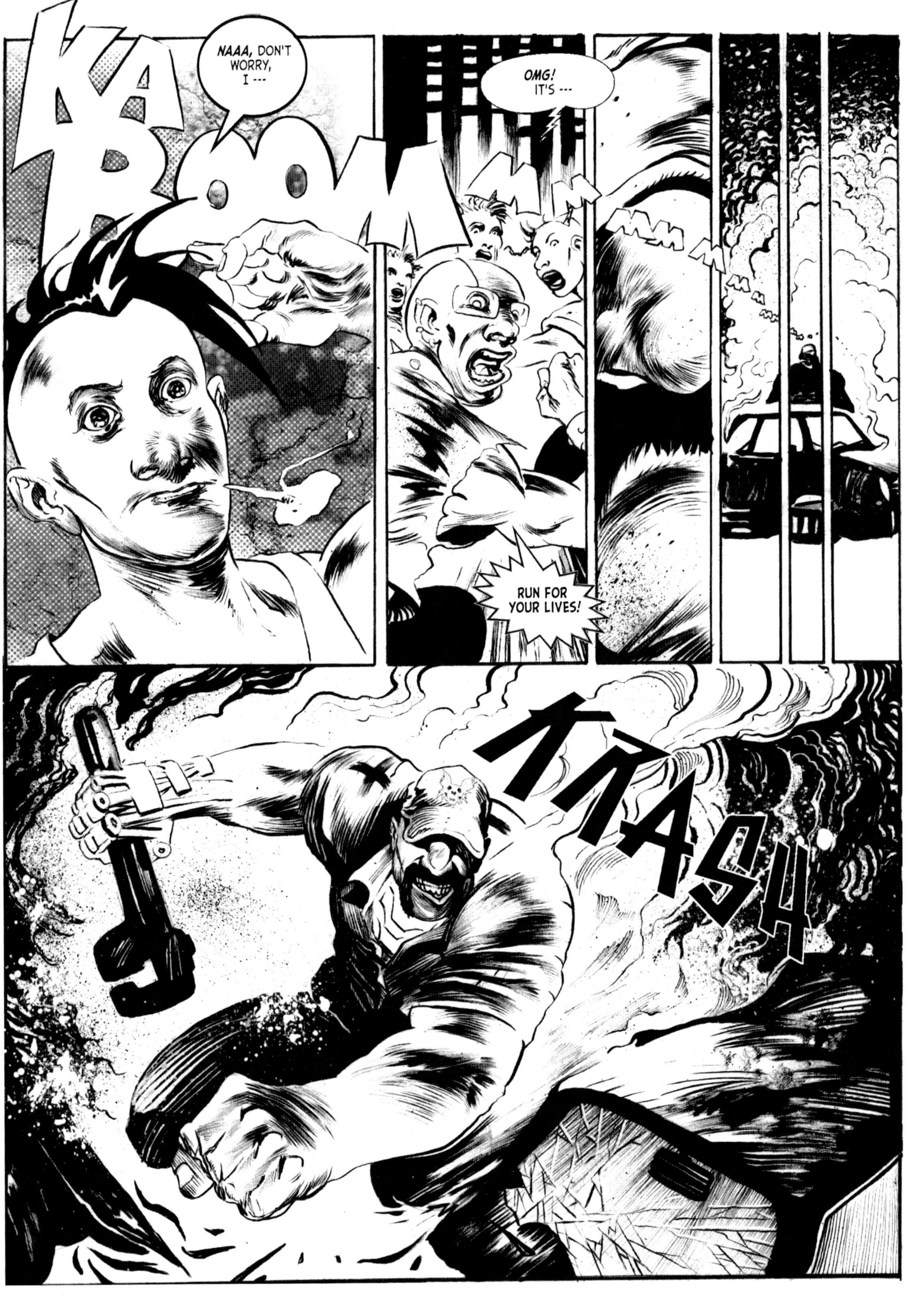
KA BOOM
NAAA, DON'T WORRY, I ---
OMG! IT'S ---
RUN FOR YOUR LIVES!
KRASH

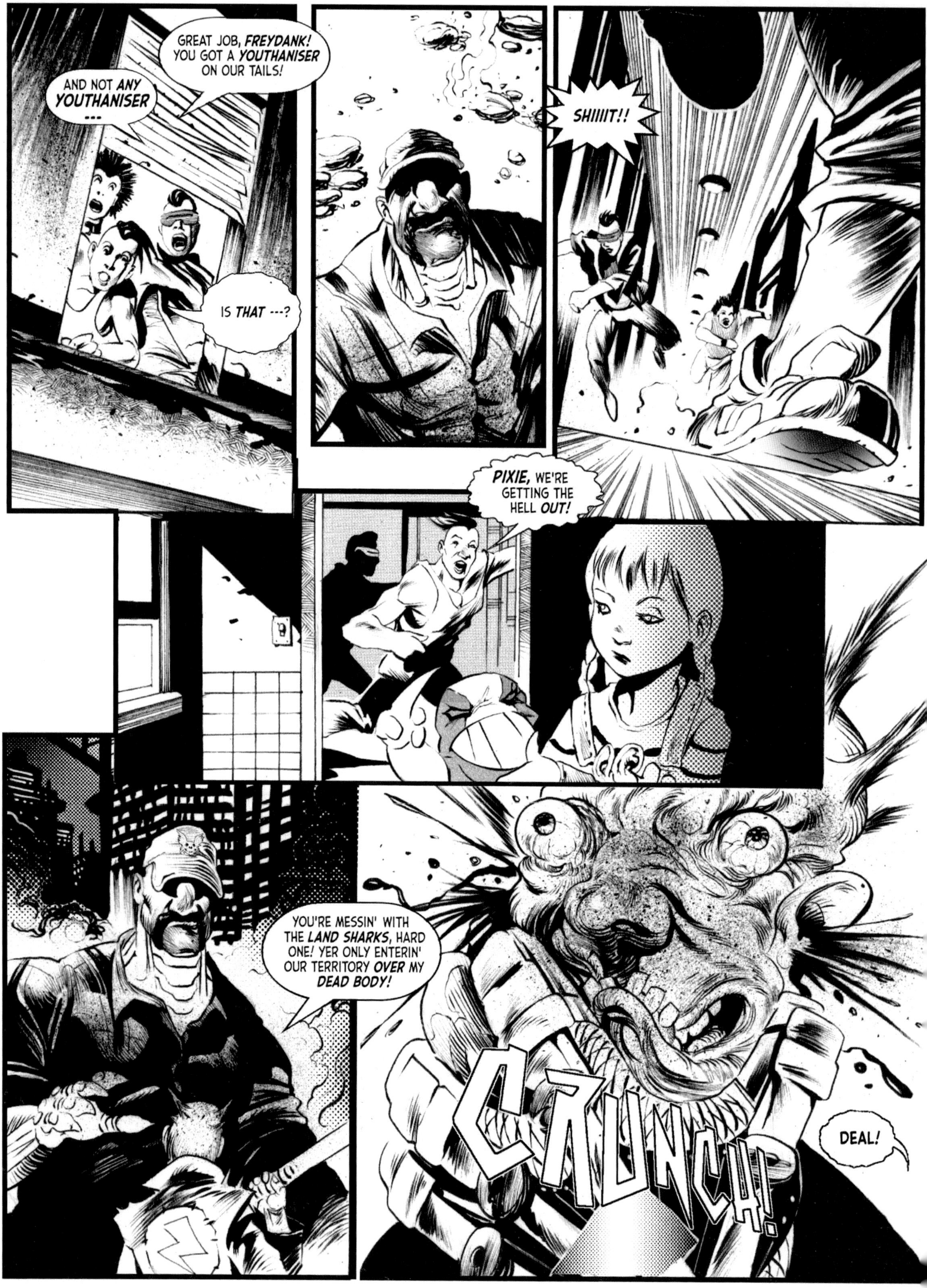
GREAT JOB, FREYDANK! YOU GOT A YOUTHANISER ON OUR TAILS!
AND NOT ANY YOUTHANISER ---
IS THAT ---?
SHIIIIT!!
PIXIE, WE'RE GETTING THE HELL OUT!
YOU'RE MESSIN' WITH THE LAND SHARKS, HARD ONE! YER ONLY ENTERIN' OUR TERRITORY OVER MY DEAD BODY!
CRUNCH!
DEAL!

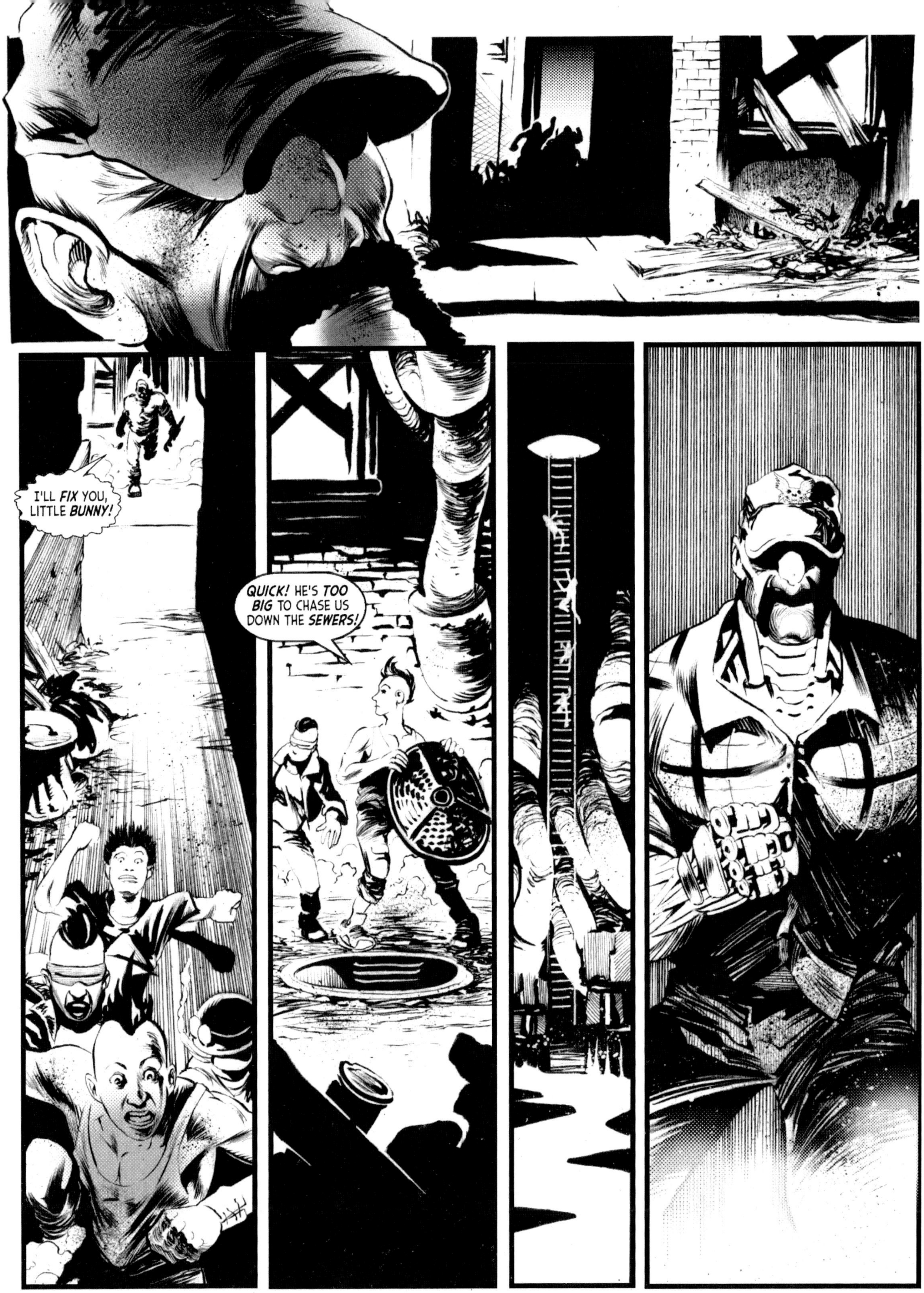
I'LL FIX YOU, LITTLE BUNNY!
QUICK! HE'S TOO BIG TO CHASE US DOWN THE SEWERS!

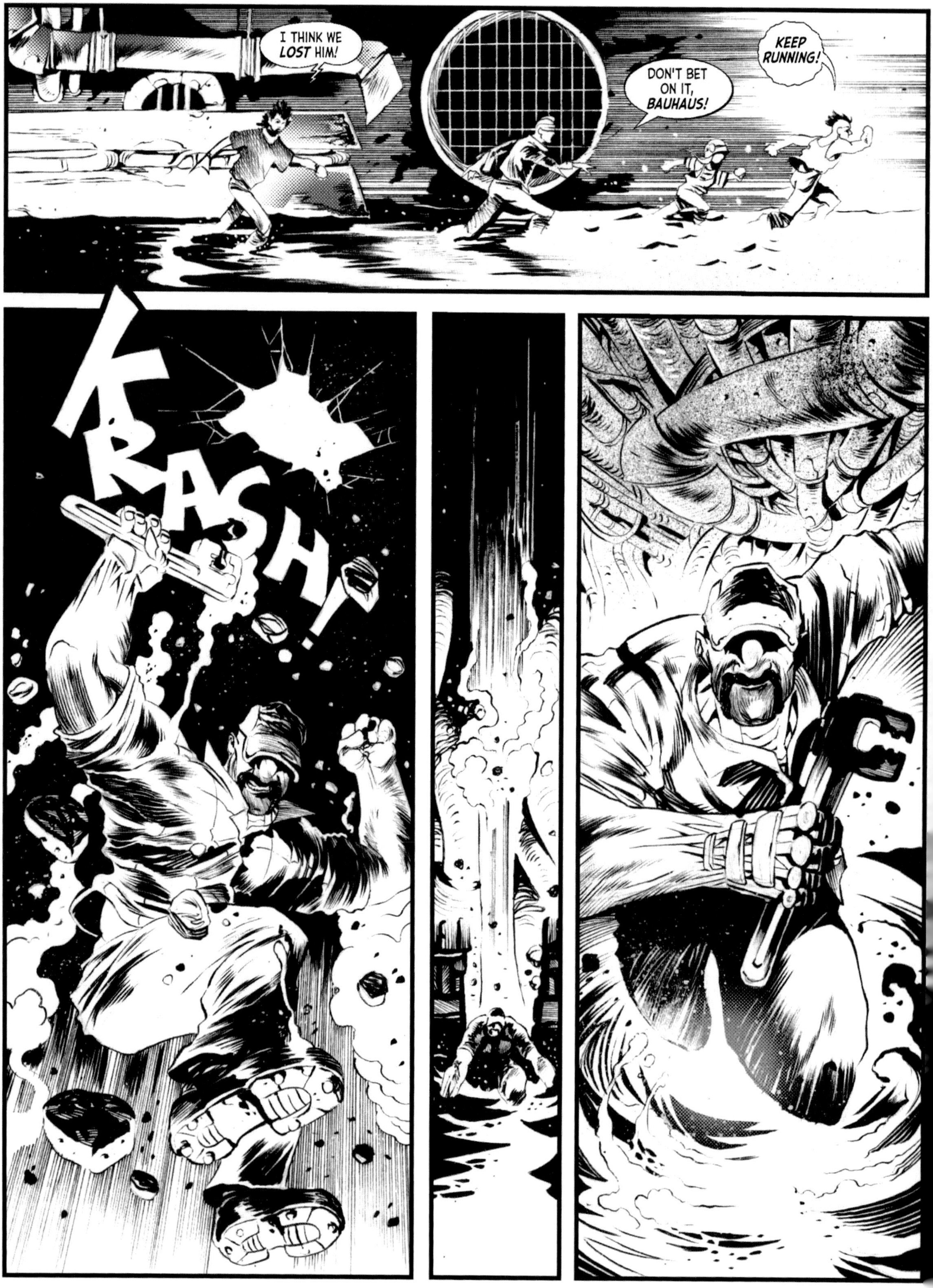
I THINK WE LOST HIM!
DON'T BET ON IT, BAUHAUS!
KEEP RUNNING!
KRASH!

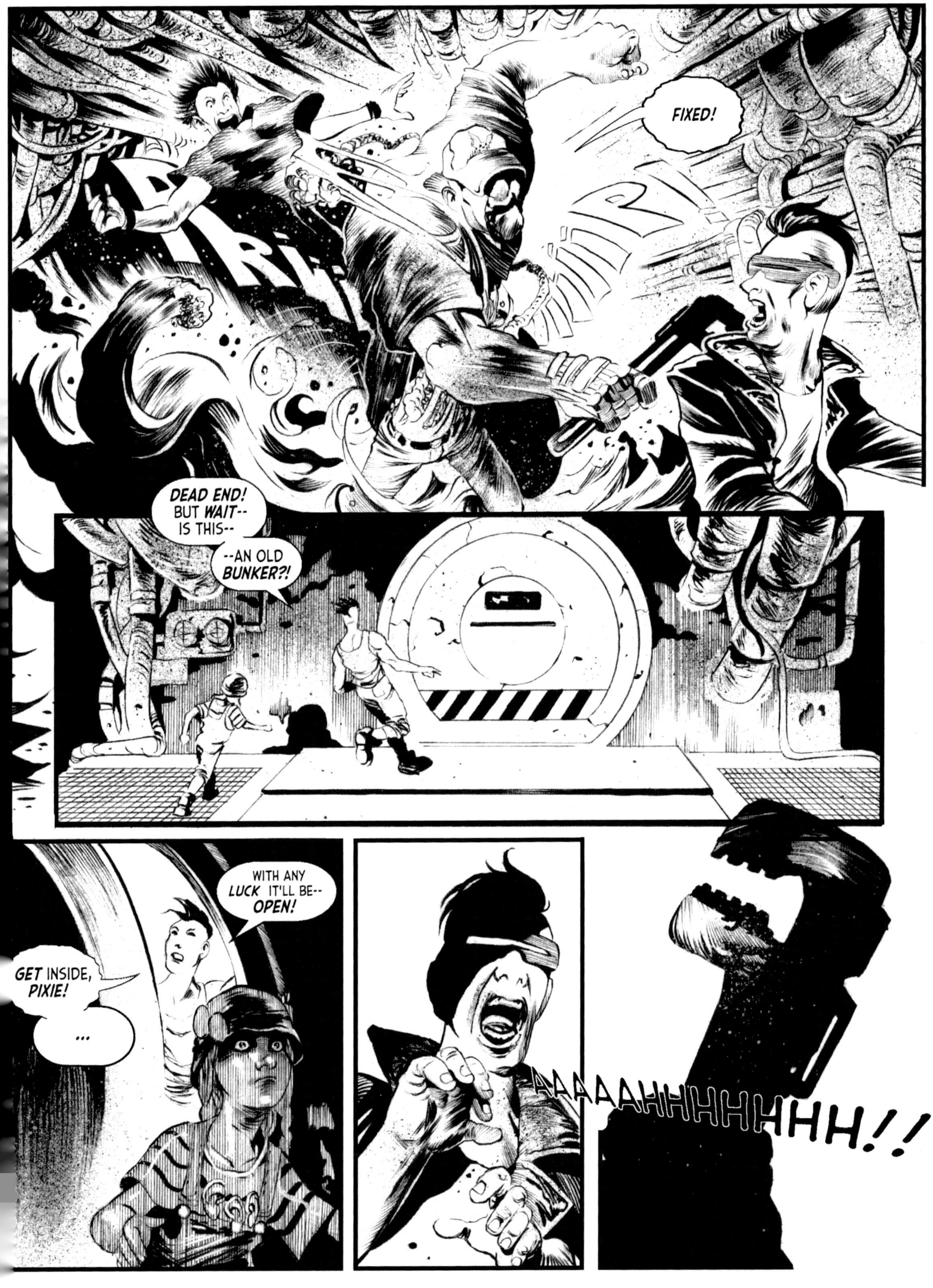
FIXED!
DEAD END! BUT WAIT-- IS THIS--
--AN OLD BUNKER?!
WITH ANY LUCK IT'LL BE-- OPEN!
GET INSIDE, PIXIE!
...
AAAAAHHHHHHHHH!!!

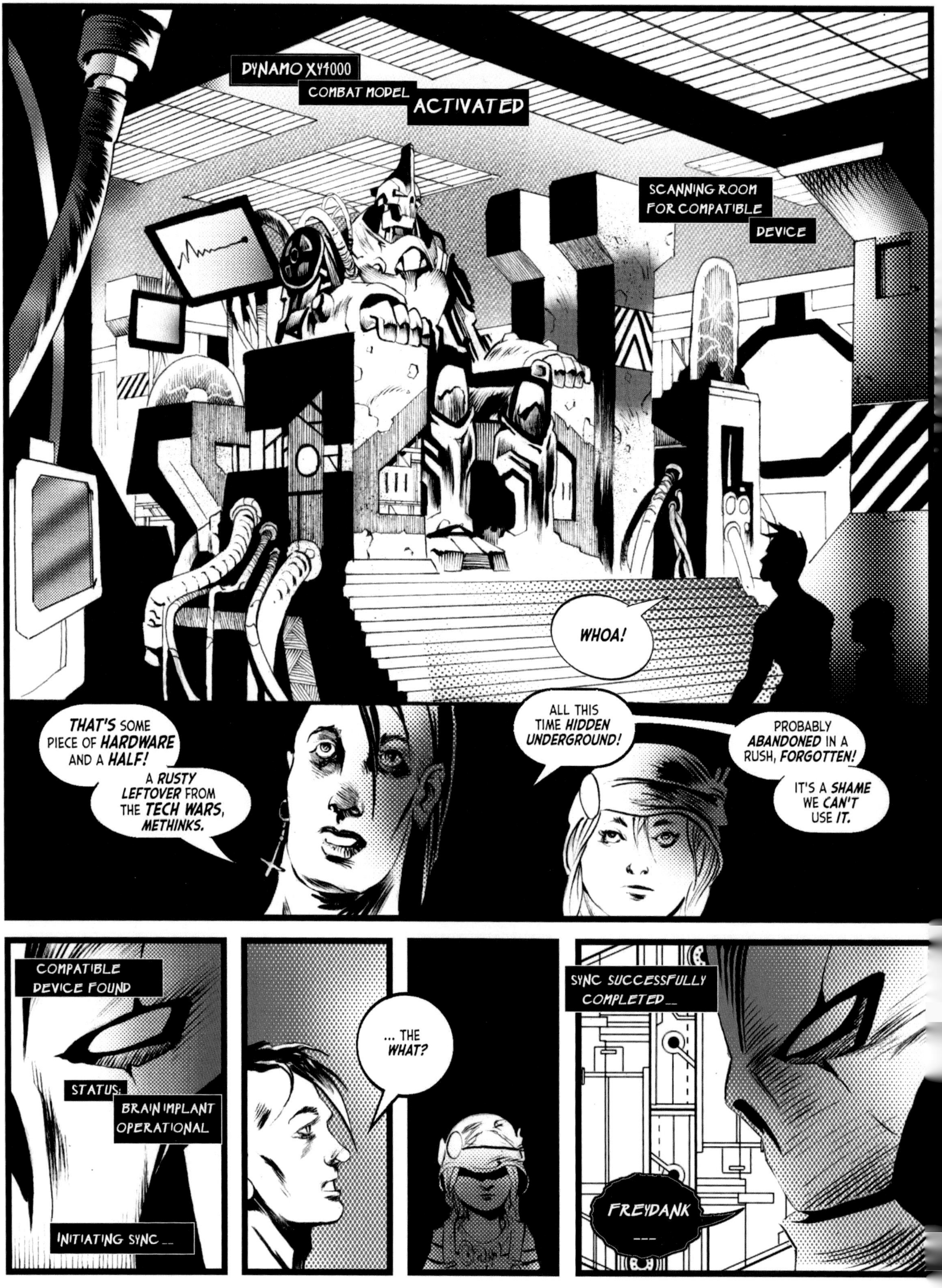
DYNAMO XY4000
COMBAT MODEL
ACTIVATED
SCANNING ROOM FOR COMPATIBLE DEVICE
WHOA!
THAT'S SOME PIECE OF HARDWARE AND A HALF!
A RUSTY LEFTOVER FROM THE TECH WARS, METHINKS.
ALL THIS TIME HIDDEN UNDERGROUND!
PROBABLY ABANDONED IN A RUSH, FORGOTTEN!
IT'S A SHAME WE CAN'T USE IT.
COMPATIBLE DEVICE FOUND
STATUS:
BRAIN IMPLANT OPERATIONAL
INITIATING SYNC __
... THE WHAT?
SYNC SUCCESSFULLY COMPLETED __
FREYDANK

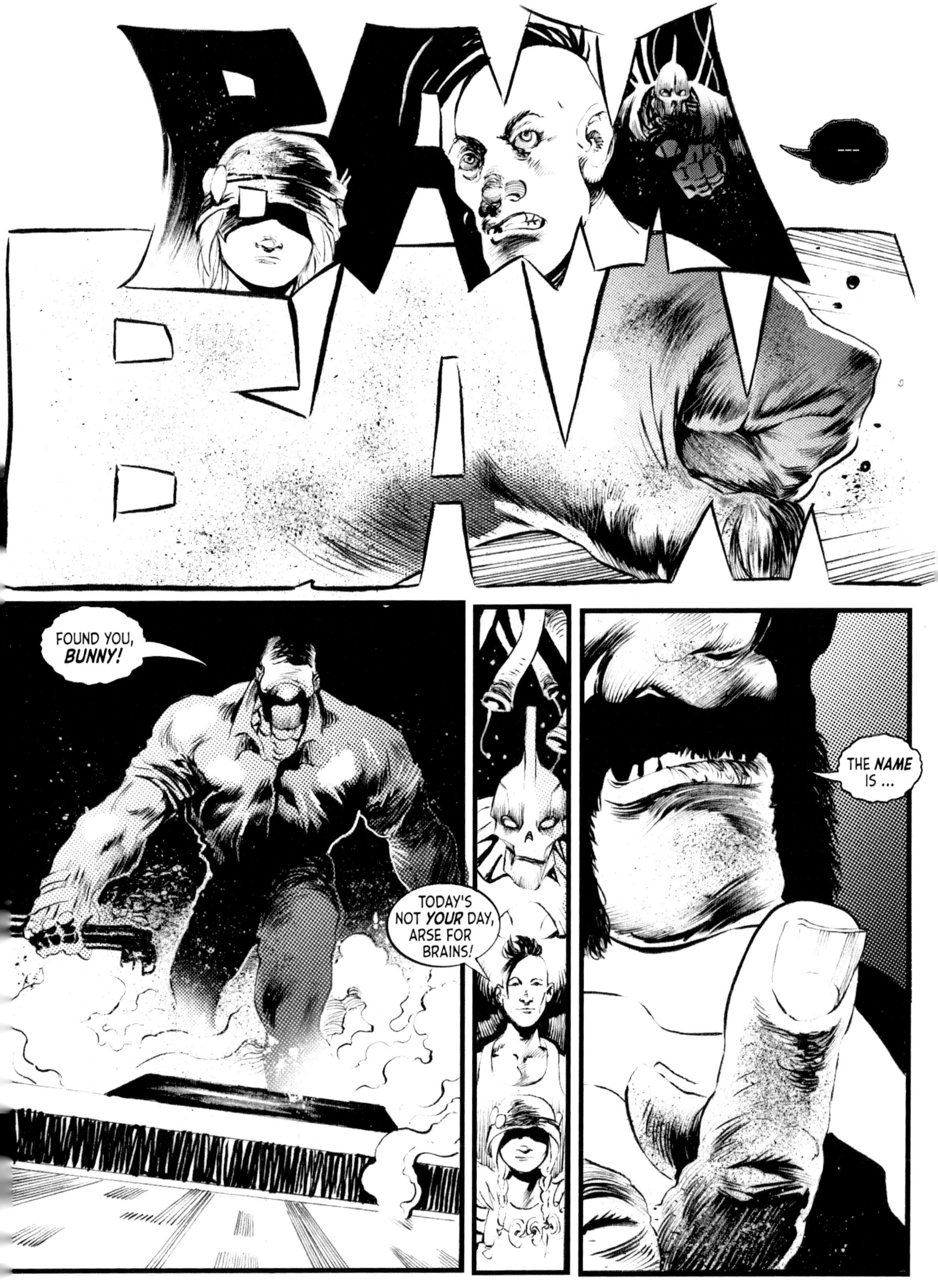
BAM BAM

FOUND YOU, *BUNNY!*
TODAY'S NOT *YOUR* DAY, ARSE FOR BRAINS!
THE *NAME* IS ...

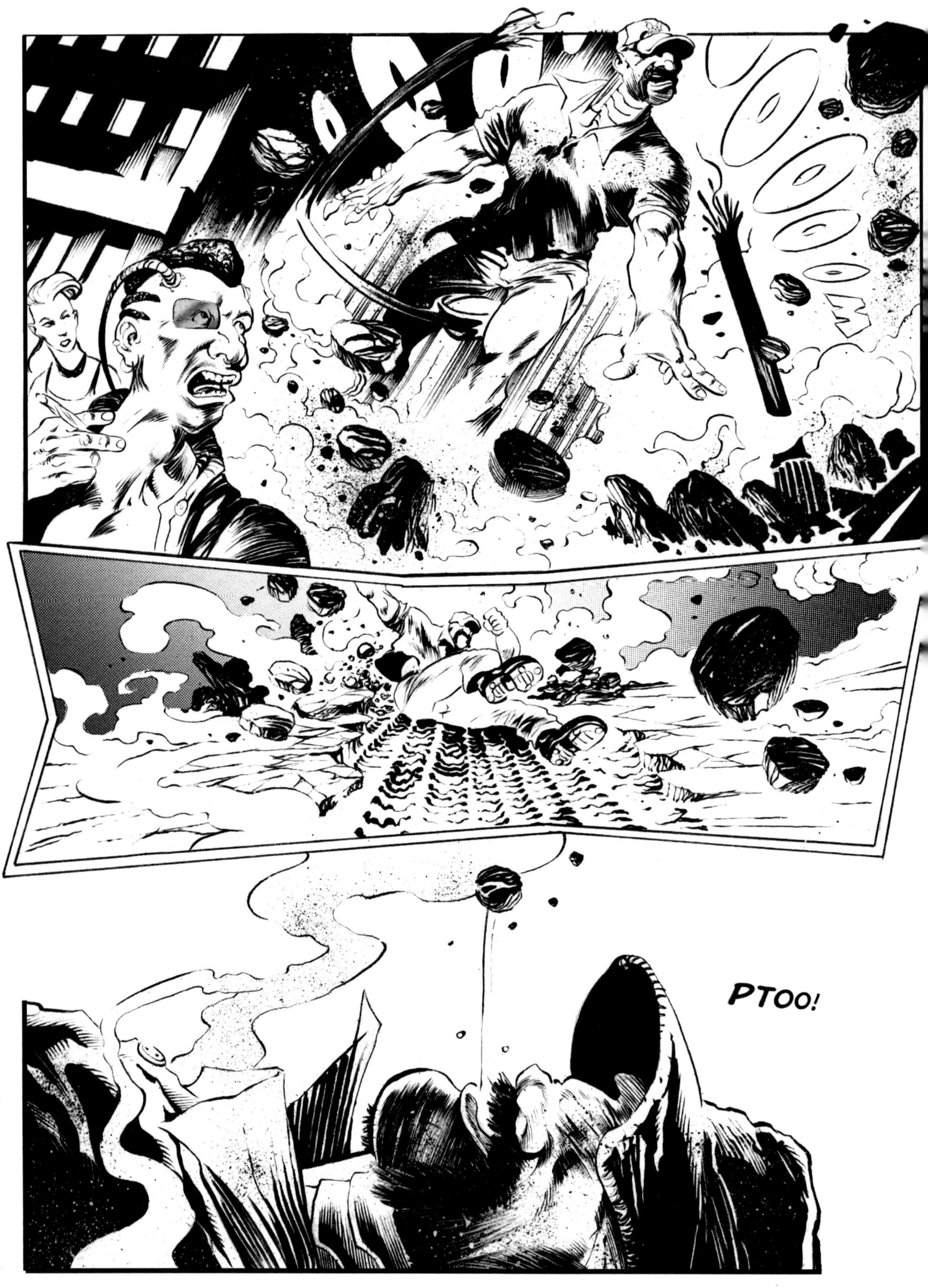
PTOO!

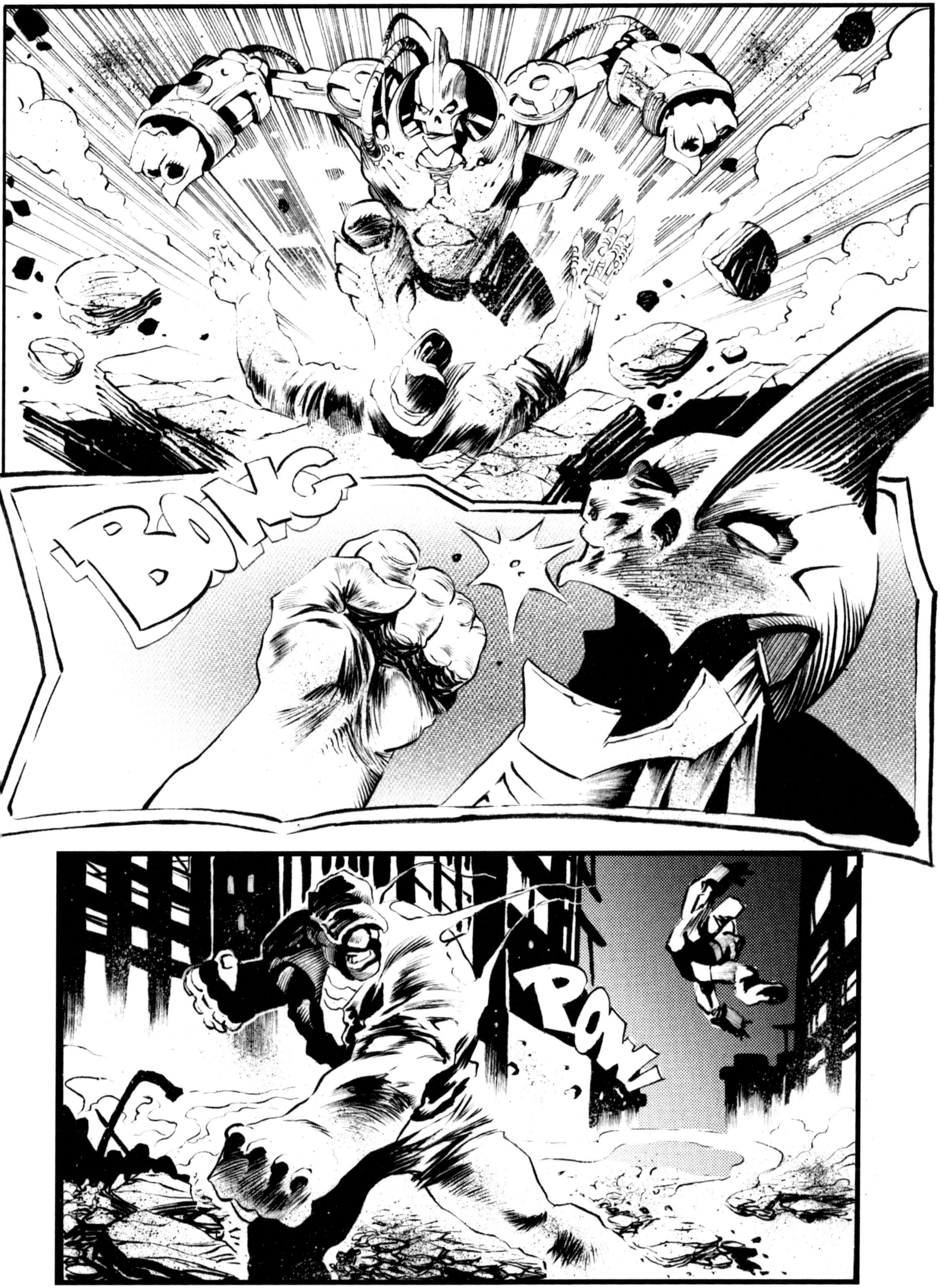
BONG
POW

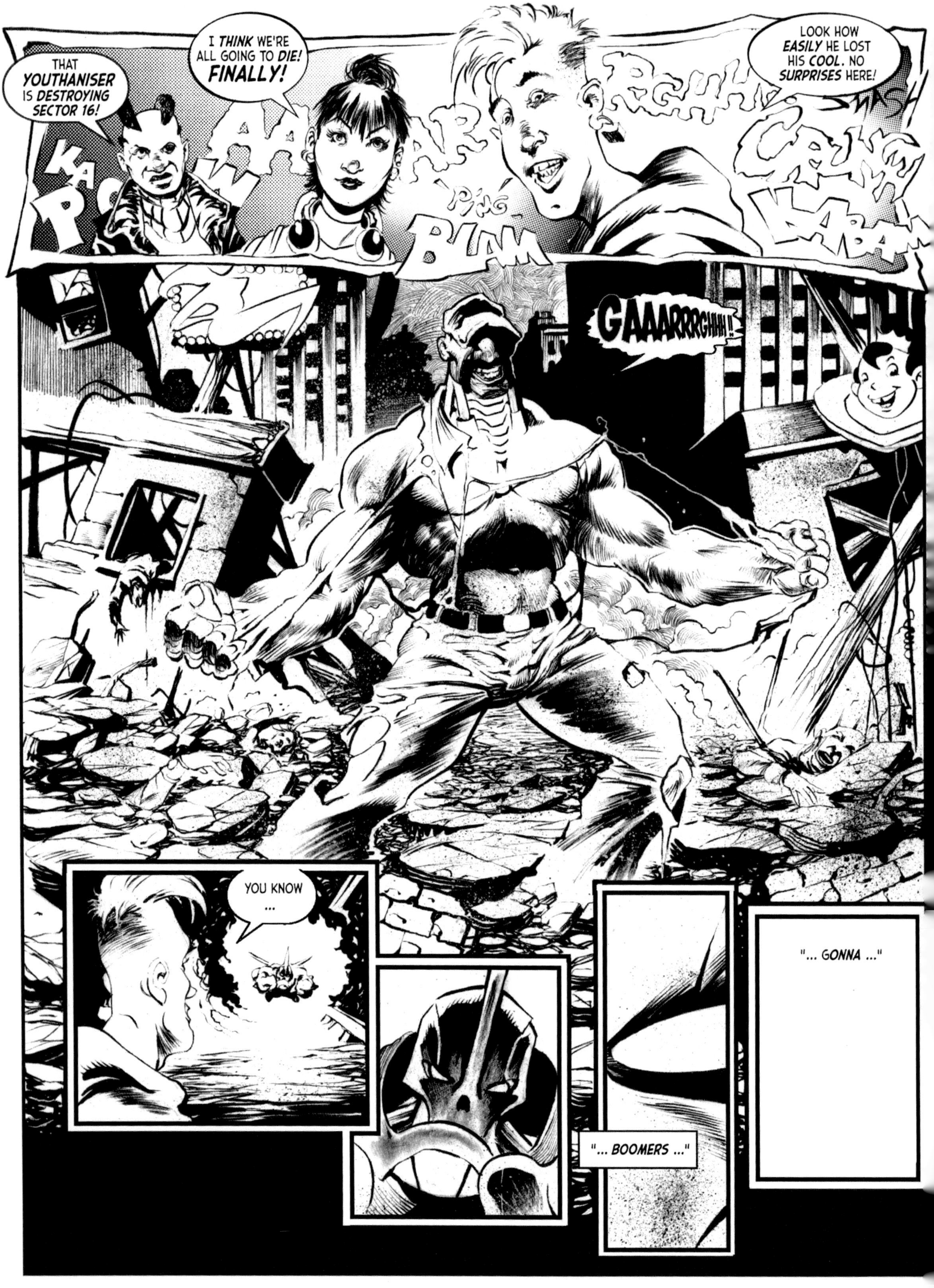
THAT YOUTHANISER IS DESTROYING SECTOR 16!
I THINK WE'RE ALL GOING TO DIE! FINALLY!
LOOK HOW EASILY HE LOST HIS COOL. NO SURPRISES HERE!
KA POW
AAARR
RGUHH
SMASH
CRUNCH
PING
BLAM
KABAM
GAAARRRGHHH!!
YOU KNOW ...
"... BOOMERS ..."
"... GONNA ..."

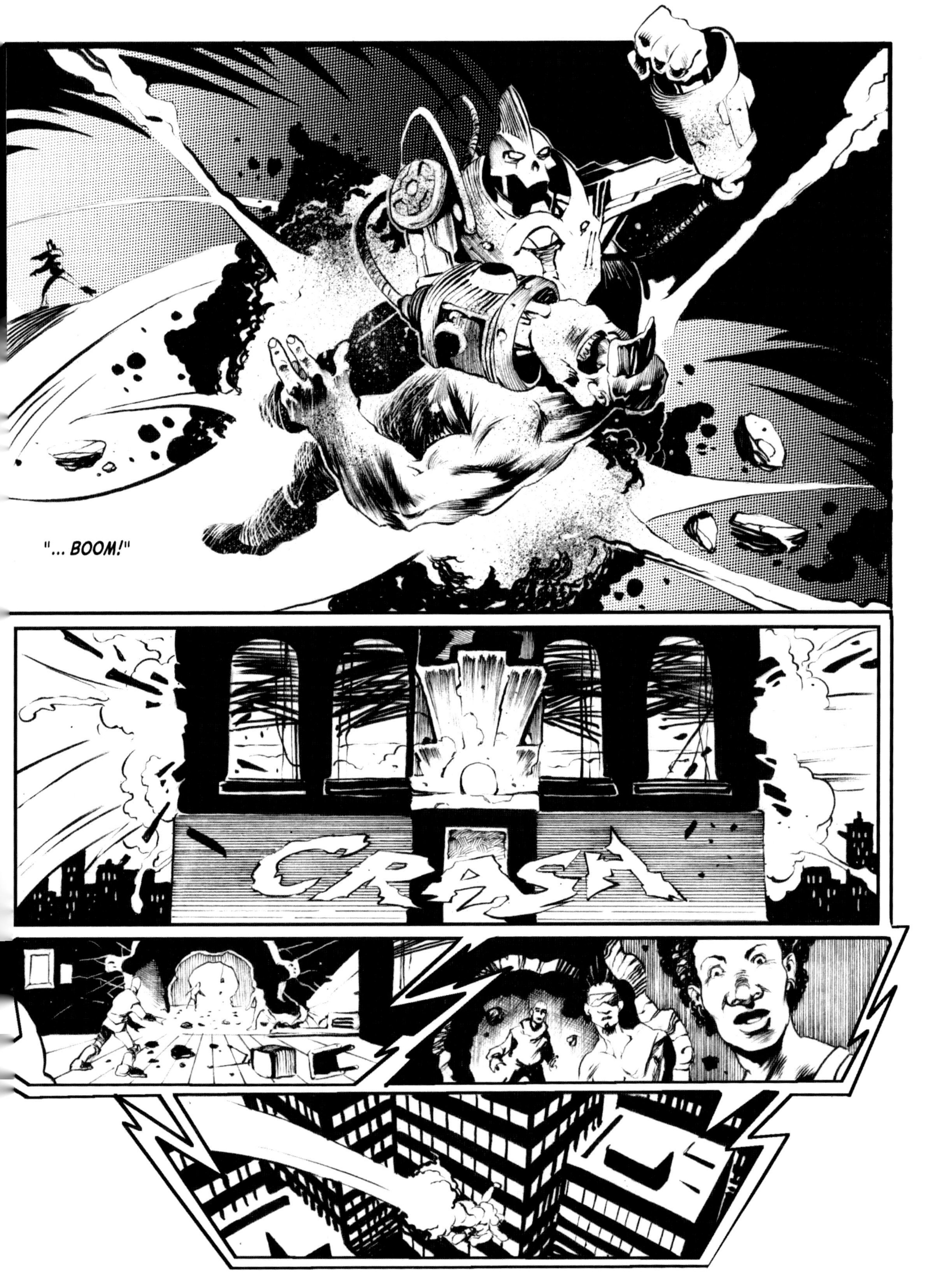
"... BOOM!"
CRASH

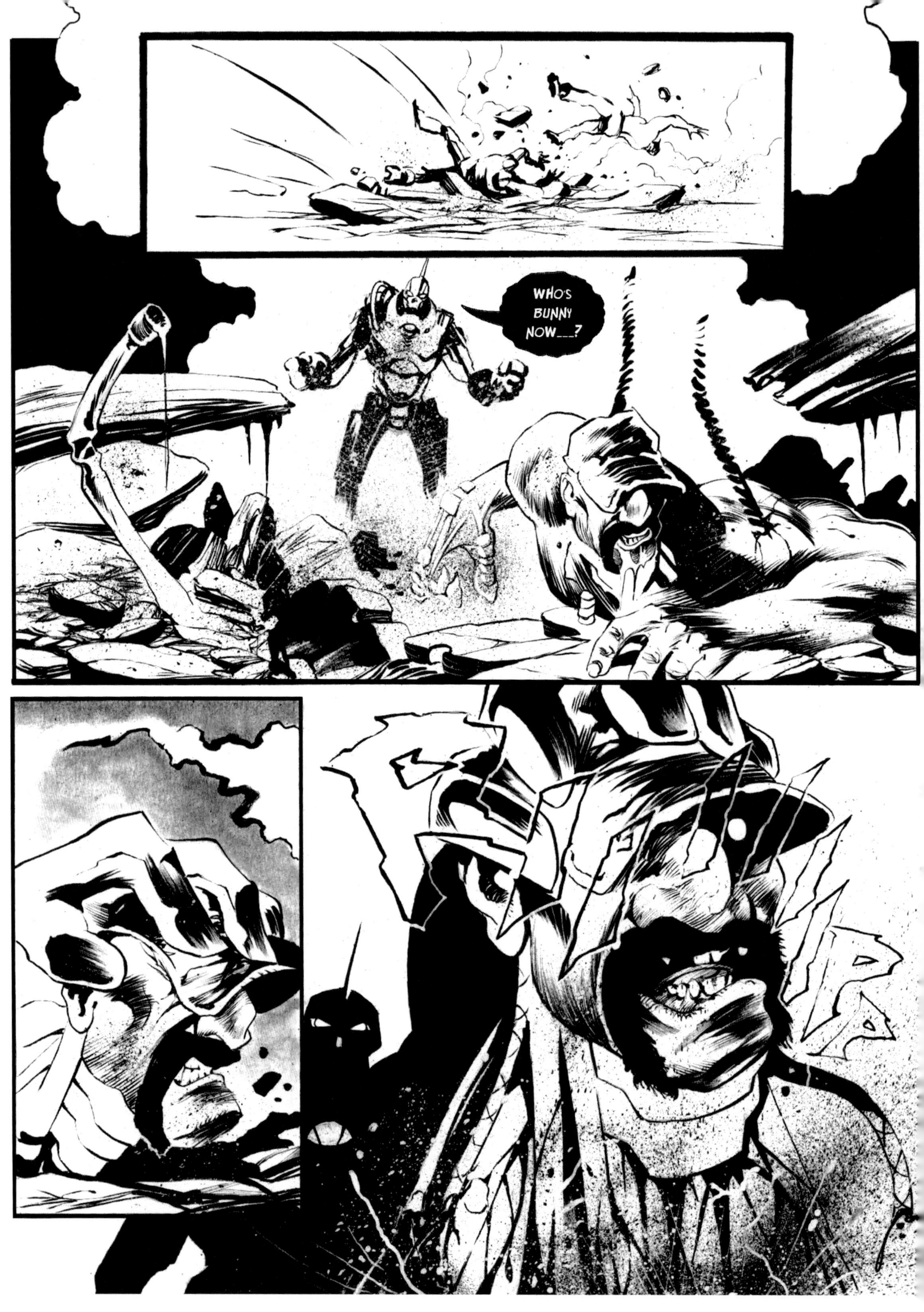
WHO'S BUNNY NOW...?

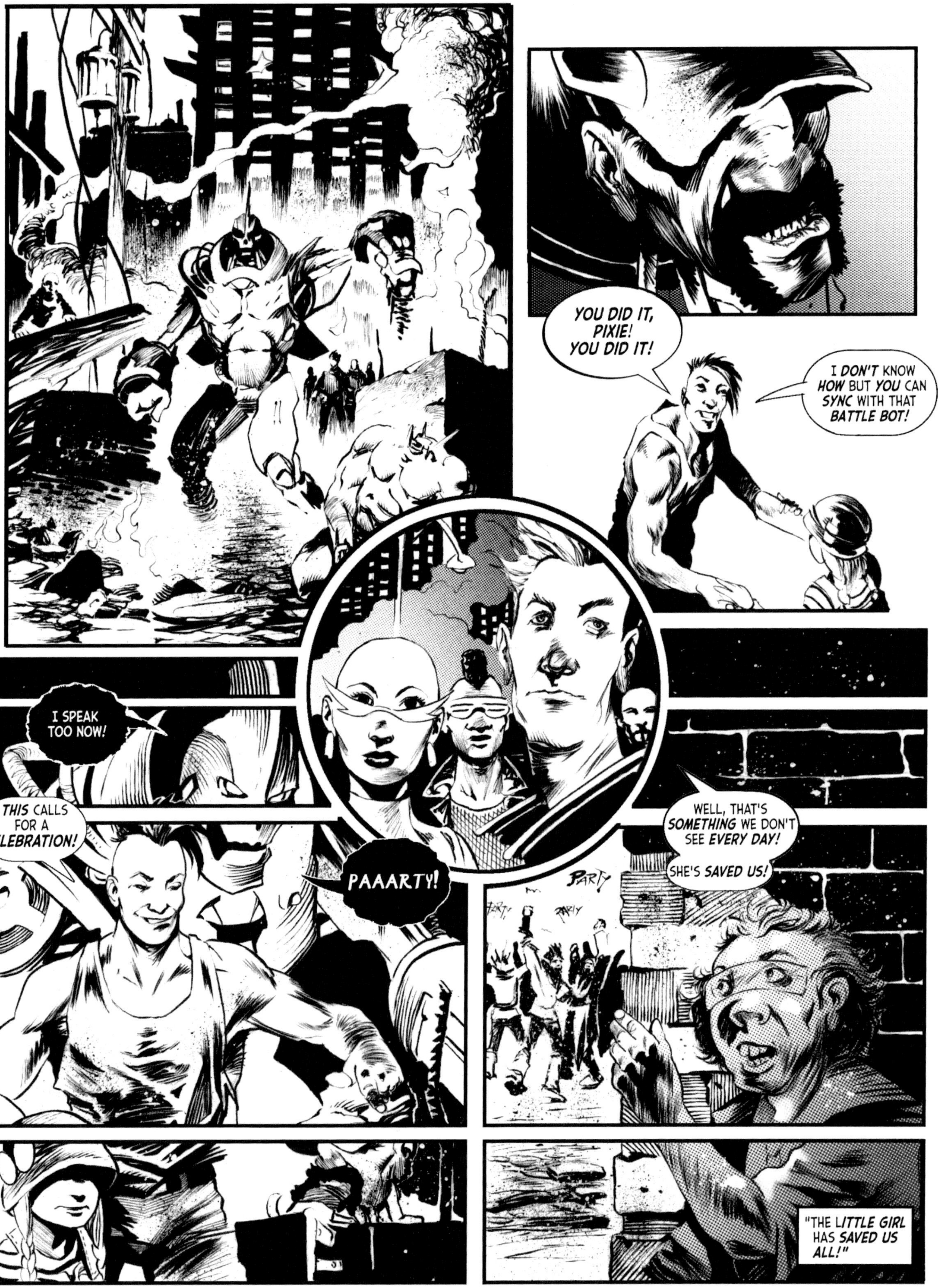
YOU DID IT, PIXIE! YOU DID IT!
I DON'T KNOW HOW BUT YOU CAN SYNC WITH THAT BATTLE BOT!
I SPEAK TOO NOW!
THIS CALLS FOR A ELEBRATION!
PAAARTY!
WELL, THAT'S SOMETHING WE DON'T SEE EVERY DAY!
SHE'S SAVED US!
PARTY
PARTY
PARTY
"THE LITTLE GIRL HAS SAVED US ALL!"

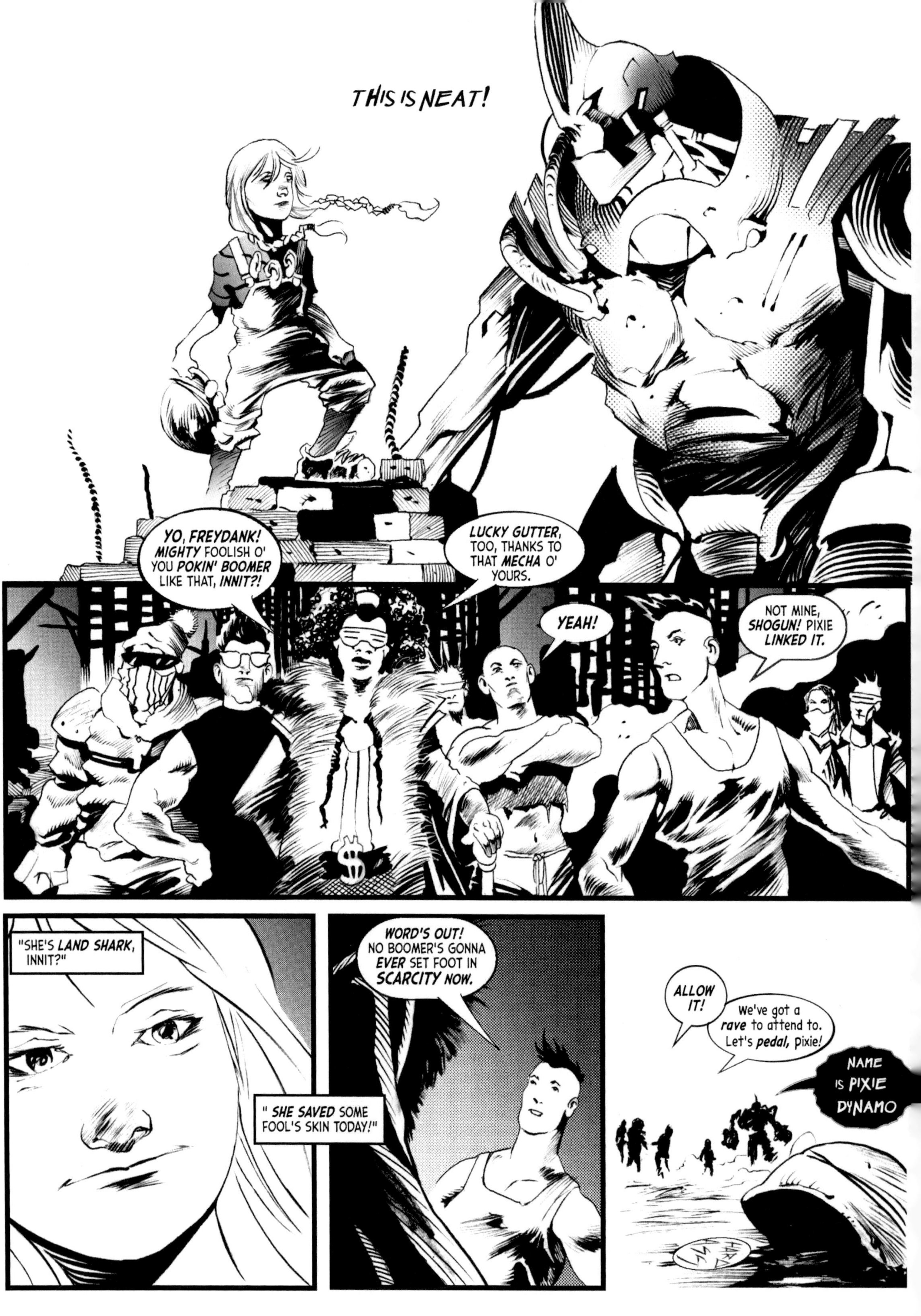

THIS IS NEAT!
YO, FREYDANK! MIGHTY FOOLISH O' YOU POKIN' BOOMER LIKE THAT, INNIT?!
LUCKY GUTTER, TOO, THANKS TO THAT MECHA O' YOURS.
YEAH!
NOT MINE, SHOGUN! PIXIE LINKED IT.
"SHE'S LAND SHARK, INNIT?"
" SHE SAVED SOME FOOL'S SKIN TODAY!"
WORD'S OUT! NO BOOMER'S GONNA EVER SET FOOT IN SCARCITY NOW.
ALLOW IT!
We've got a rave to attend to. Let's pedal, pixie!
NAME IS PIXIE DYNAMO

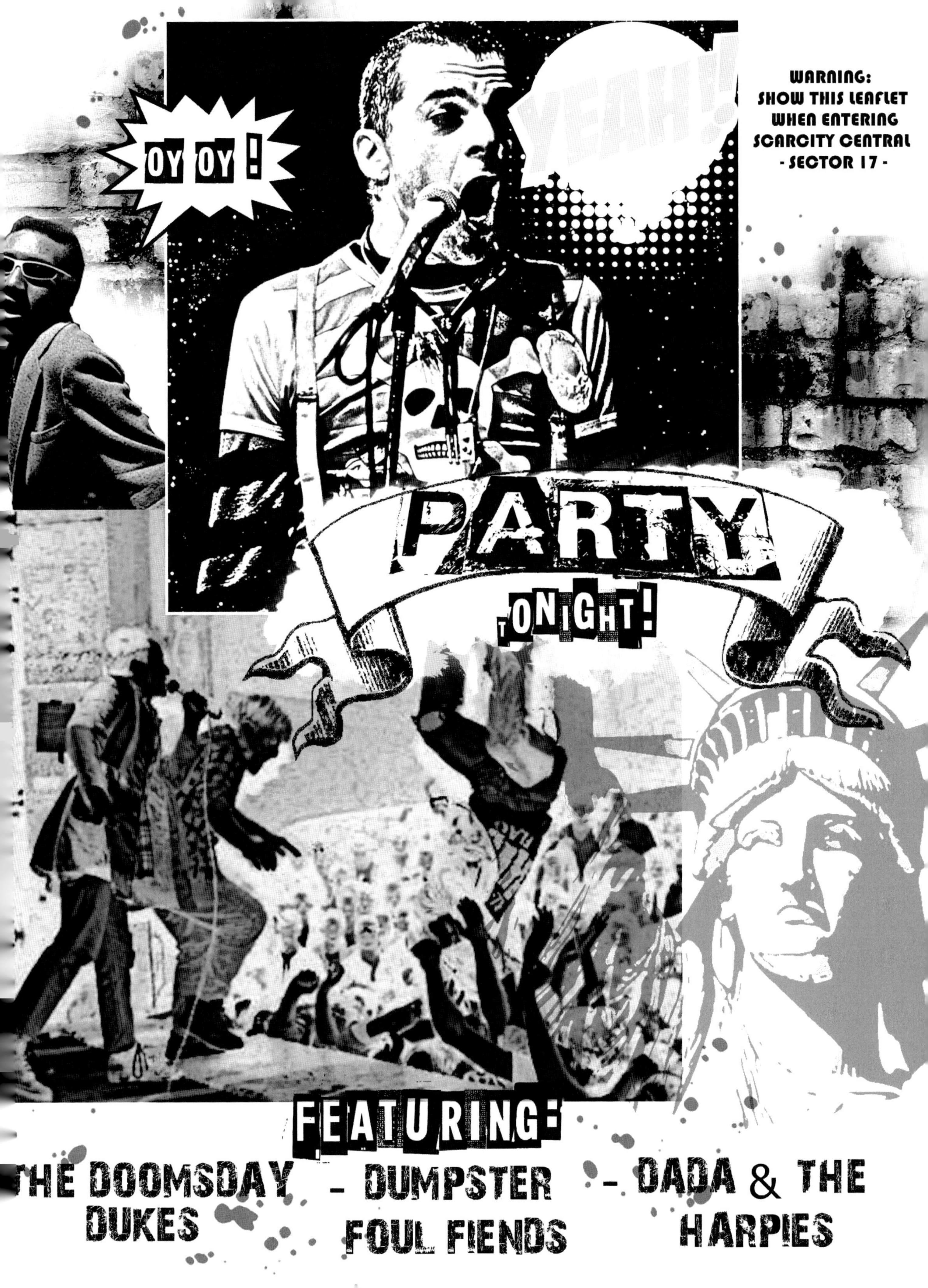
OY OY !
YEAH!!
WARNING:
SHOW THIS LEAFLET
WHEN ENTERING
SCARCITY CENTRAL
- SECTOR 17 -
PARTY
TONIGHT!
FEATURING:
THE DOOMSDAY DUKES
- DUMPSTER FOUL FIENDS
- DADA & THE HARPIES

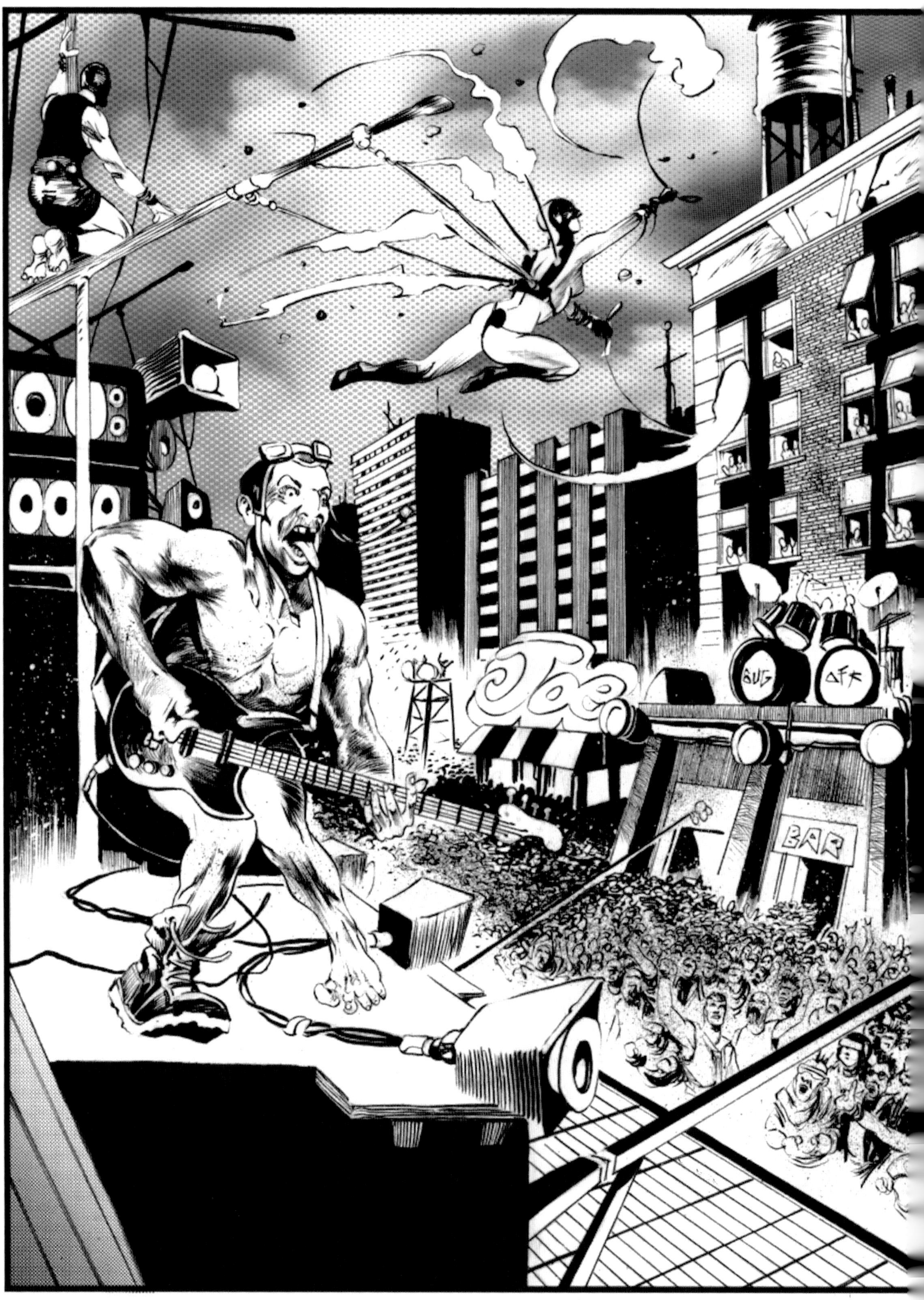
Joe
BUG
OFF
BAR

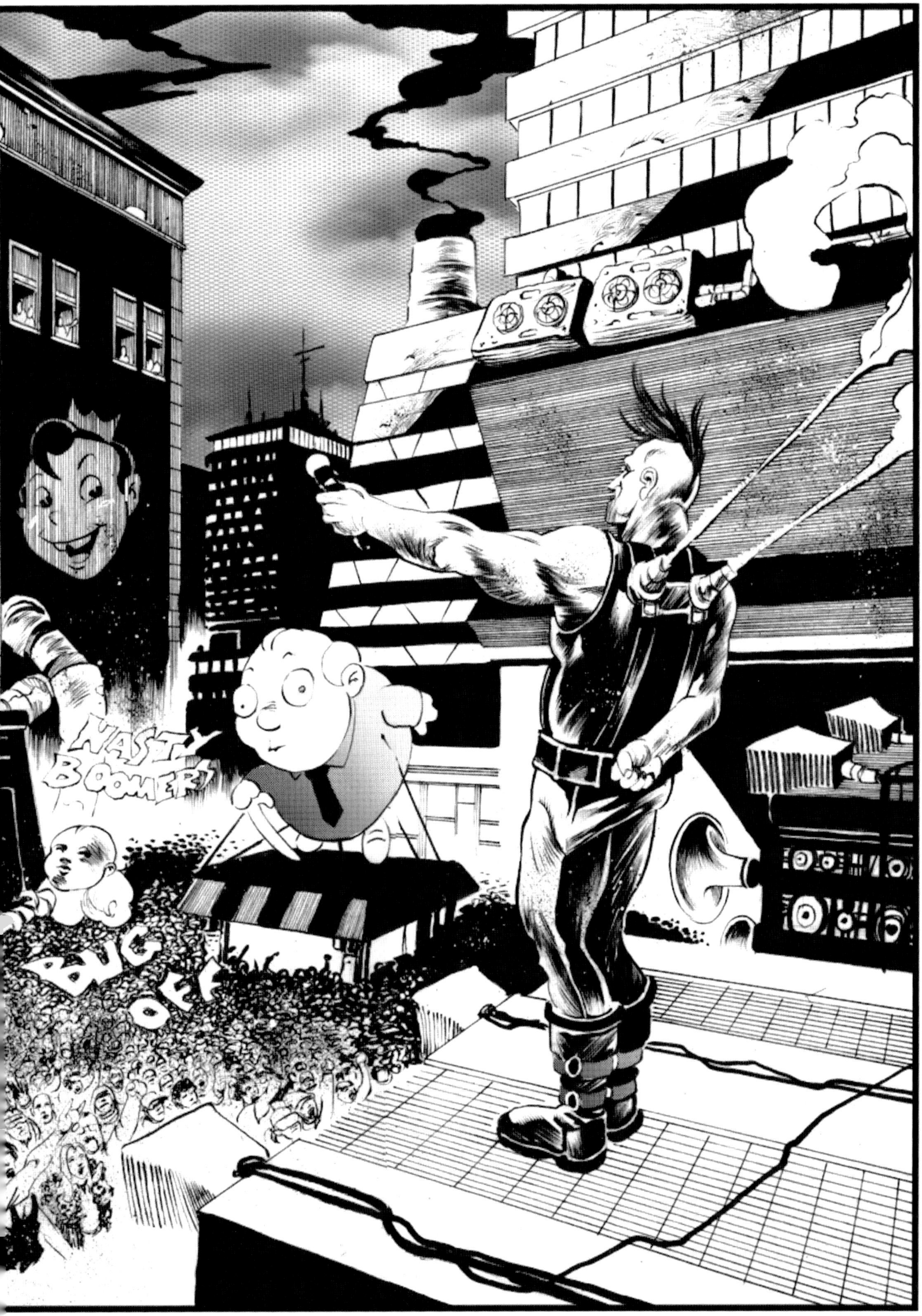
NASTY BOOMERS

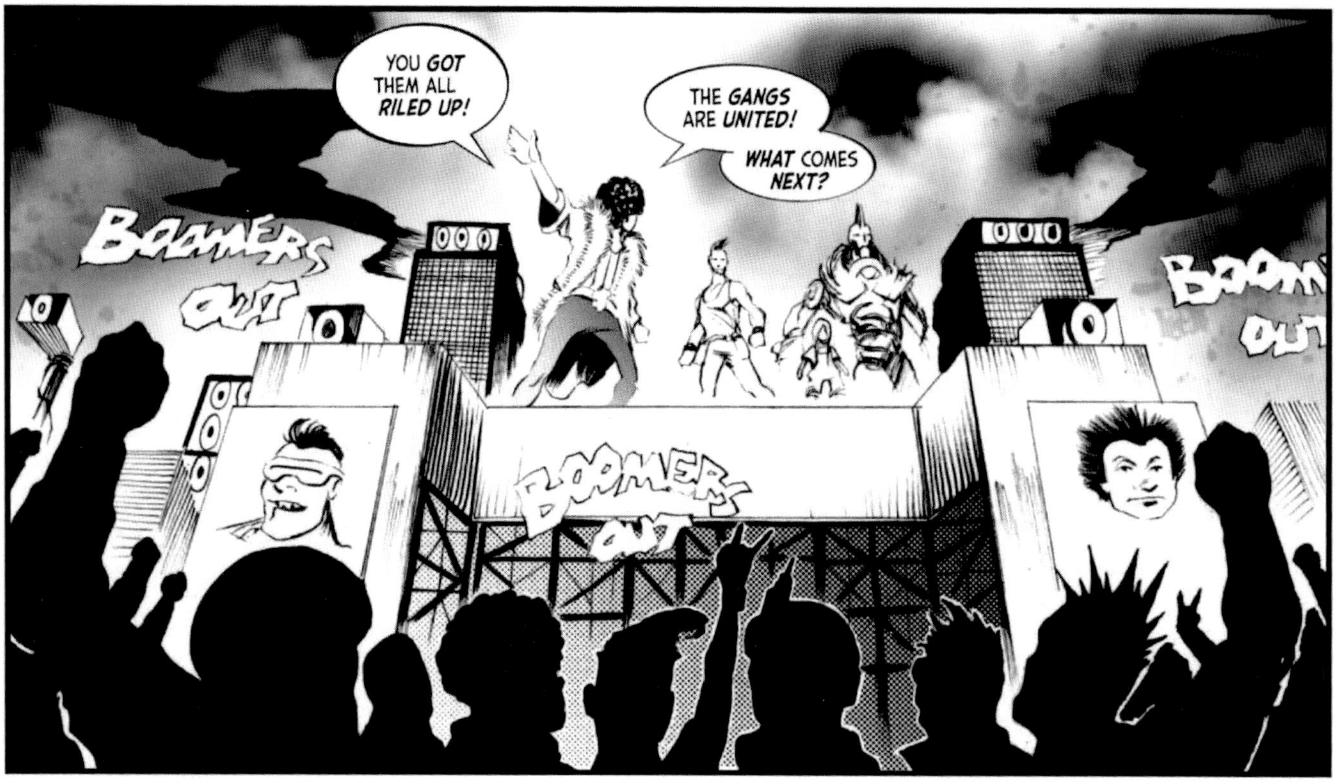
BOOMERS OUT
YOU GOT THEM ALL RILED UP!
THE GANGS ARE UNITED!
WHAT COMES NEXT?
BOOMERS OUT

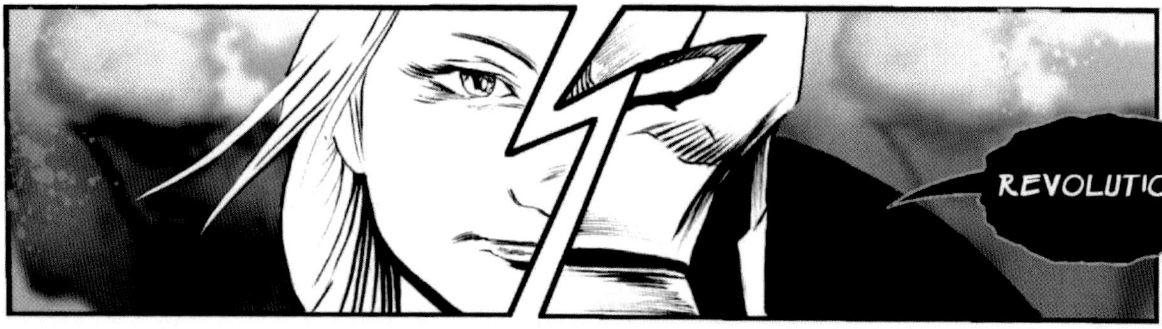
REVOLUTION!

WRITTEN AND
ILLUSTRATED BY

BRUNO STAHL